NEW COUNTRY TALK

ILLUSTRATED BY B. S. BIRO, FSIA

NEW COUNTRY TALK

J. H. B. PEEL

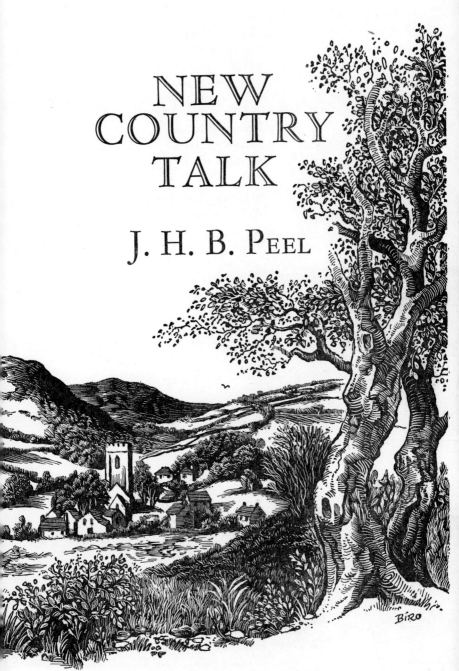

ROBERT HALE · LONDON

Printed in Great Britain by
Ebenezer Baylis and Son, Limited
The Trinity Press, Worcester, and London

Contents

Contents

Contents

A*

I have a commonplace book for facts and
another for poetry, but I find it difficult always
to preserve the vague distinction . . .

Henry David Thoreau

I

Leaning on a Gate

Five-barred gates exist primarily in order to confine livestock. How remarkable, therefore, that they should fit the measurements of the man who likes to lean his elbows on a ledge while admiring the view or pondering the verities. In a longish life of gate-leaning I have never yet encountered an uppermost bar that was uncomfortably high or excessively low. Every five-barred gate seems to have been designed as a wayside resting place. I refer, of course, to timber gates, not to those metal tubes which some commercial townsman devised for the benefit of people who prefer the cheap and nasty. Such gates mock the wayfarer seeking a shelf for his map and his sandwiches. They clang, moreover, and the whine of their hinge sets the teeth on edge. They are lifeless, as all metal is lifeless, and the rust stains whatever it touches. In short, metal gates reek of the factory. A timber gate, by contrast, was once a living tree. When properly maintained, the gate swings sedately, and shuts with a crisp click. The man who made it may still be alive. If you look closely you will see where his hammer struck, and where the blade went. Walter Rose, a village carpenter at Haddenham in Buckinghamshire, wrote: "The making of a gate was considered a day's work for a qualified carpenter, and was expected to be done in the ten hours which at that time constituted a day of labour . . . A field gate so made of good English heart oak would last the greater part of a lifetime . . . My father frequently pointed out to me a gate that he had made fifty years ago."

Having no life, a metal gate has no lifestory. The factory manager could not tell you when the first process began nor where the last ended. He could not even name the site at which the ore had been mined. Timber gates, on the other hand, really do possess a family tree; and sometimes their genealogy can be traced *ab initio*, as, for example, when a Suffolk farmer showed me the genesis of his own gate. First, he led me to the stump of an oak. Then he introduced me to the man who had felled that oak. In a sunny corner of the yard we saw where the timber had been seasoned for three years; and after that we strolled into the village, to meet the carpenter and the farrier who made the gate, and the youth who helped to hang it. On our return a small boy pointed to the gate, saying proudly: "My grampa made that 'un." Is there in Luton, or Coventry, or Oxford a child who could boast: "My mum's boyfriend sprayed that nearside wing"?

A gate can be both solitary and companionable; intrinsically contemplative and conversational. At dawn it supports Wordsworth's traveller,

> On Man, on Nature, and on Human Life
> Musing in solitude . . .

At noon it becomes a rendezvous for farmers, beaglers, holidaymakers, and any others who chance to meet there, leaning and looking while they pass the time of day. At night it welcomes the whispering lovers, or perhaps a farmer who, while he stares at the stars, states a mystery by asking a question: "What is man, that thou art mindful of him?" Such gate-leaning is the reverse of clock-watching, because it forgets the time, and is immersed in Coleridge's "Sabbath of self-content". Had Archimedes conducted his experiments at a pond, he might have been leaning on the gate, instead of reclining in the bath, when he cried "Eureka!" Was it while leaning on a gate—maybe in his beloved

Kent—that Dickens "thought of Mr Pickwick"? It was certainly while leaning on a gate near Pond Farm in the Chiltern hamlet of Great Hampden that Masefield composed part of *The Everlasting Mercy*, the poem which marked him as a potential Laureate. He told me so himself, and afterwards I went to see whether the gate still stood. "No," said the farmer. "We replaced it in the 1930s. But considering my grandfather bought it during the Crimean War, I think we received value for money."

What gates there are in Britain! What vistas they command! If you travel as far north as you can, without stepping into the Pentland Firth, you may find the gate on which I leaned while the waves were stippled with stars, and a ship winked her port light en route for the Orkneys. If you travel as far west as you can, without stepping into the Atlantic Ocean, you may find the gate on which I leaned while the waves made their landfall at Land's End, and dawn rode red-sailed on a rising tide. In the wilds of Exmoor lies a grass track, hollowed by man and beast through incalculable years. Very old people can remember a time when the track served a farm, but today the house is a ruin, the garden is a grave, the shippon is a wreck. The gate, however, stands intact, though scarcely recognisable as the oak from which it was made, being green with moss, rain, wind, sun, snow, and with whatever hidden katabolism causes all things in their season to decay. So old is this gate that the years have thinned it, as though they were an adze silently paring the surface. And to that erosion was added a multiplicity of audible assaults, for birds have pecked it, sheep have rubbed it, carts have bumped it, men have slammed it. There is not any mood which this gate failed to see and hear, and sometimes to heal. Children have swung on it, farmhands have carved on it, women have wept on it. Bedsteads have passed through it, brand-new for a bride. Coffins have passed over it, shoulder-high among snowdrifts. Toddlers have reached it on their first unaided journey; and so have veterans on their last. To the families who lived at the farm, this gate was alpha and omega, their setting out and their coming home.

Climate and altitude make it difficult to estimate the gate's age; but having seen gates that were eighty years old, I would not feel surprised if this one had been hung during the last years of Queen Victoria's reign. Oak, after all, is a tough commodity, able to sail the sea on its hundredth birthday. If, therefore, this gate is handled with the consideration due to age, it may outlive the shepherd who now leans on it, counting his sheep.

A Man in Authority

He was celebrating Plough Monday by steering a straight furrow. His uniform consisted of tweed jacket and cap, and gumboots over jodhpurs. When strangers are informed that he is seventy years old they refuse to believe it, at any rate until they have approached near enough to notice the tracery of lines at the corner of his eyes. Then they exclaim: "He's either a farmer or a sailor." In fact, he is both, having been invalided after wounds received when his destroyer engaged an Italian cruiser.

Like many other mariners, the Commander beached himself within sight of the sea that was his calling and is still his recreation. There he works a fifty-hour week, farming a small property as he commanded his ship, which is to say rigorously, justly, and with a flair that transcends mere efficiency. Some farms in the district are unkempt, but on the Commander's land everything is shipshape. You never see a plough capsized in midfield nor a sheet of tin plugging a broken hedge. Other farmers fasten their gates with twine, but the Commander's gates are painted white, and the latch is greased.

No industrial disputes trouble the farm, chiefly because the two part-time hands are industrious, being respectively an ex-Marine, aged sixty-five, and the Commander's former steward, aged sixty-six (known as "Hobbly" because he lost a leg at Dunkirk). To watch the three veterans working alongside is to perceive the brotherhood of man and the difference between men. They indulge neither familiarity nor contempt, but follow the rule of the sea whereby one commands, and all obey. If neighbouring farmers complain that their own men are lazy or negligent, the Commander smiles, and says nothing. When he does speak, it is briefly, dryly, conclusively; a gift which enabled him to serve with distinction on the County Council. According to the Clerk, the Commander's maiden speech began with the words: "To get back to the point..." Yet the Clerk himself allowed that the Commander was consistently courteous: "He never lost his temper. And that's saying a lot, because he was once a man in authority, and it must be hard for him to suffer people who are sometimes insolent." The Clerk might have added that the Commander keeps his best sherry for a political opponent with whom he frequently exchanged salvos across the Council chamber. Few men so forthright have made such a large number of friends and such a negligible number of enemies. Nevertheless, the Commander's *bonhomie* is not limitless. When, for example, he received an invitation to a dinner whose principal speaker was a professional trouble-maker, he declined, saying: "I am not obliged to sup with the enemies of my country."

While the vicar was writing a history of the parish, he consulted the Commander, and expressed surprise at his erudition; to which the sailor replied: "Dartmouth was by way of being a school. Of course, I never specialised. Mathematics, history, geography, English literature, French, and a bit of Latin... that's about all... except for those damned general knowledge papers. But when I was a Lieutenant I did become interested in Roman agriculture. That led to Virgil." He knew quite a bit about apple trees. In fact, I call him the first of the Pomeranians. But if he were alive in England now, I doubt that he'd say "*O fortunatos agricolas*. I've just sold some beef cattle because I can't afford to feed 'em. And how much do you think they fetched? I'll tell you... it was less than I paid for 'em."

All men are imperfect; and many dispute the nature of

perfection. To some, therefore, it will seem a merit, to others a defect, that the Commander speaks his mind. Arriving one night at Euston, and finding no one to help him with the luggage, he turned to a group of employees who were playing cards on an upturned trolley: "Hey, you there!" he shouted. "Come and do something useful." And, of course, there was the famous occasion when he reminded the electorate that in Vietnam the Americans were resisting aggression; whereupon a heckler shouted "Warmonger!" The Commander replied: "I joined the Royal Navy as a cadet at the age of twelve. But I have yet to meet the sailor who wished to get killed."

His frankness, however, is tempered with tact, which together mark his wide and active interests. Besides being church warden and secretary of the Hunt, he is steward of the annual point-to-point and treasurer of the local British Legion. He also takes a keen interest in the village Youth Centre, to which he lends his dinghy for weekend sailing. "There's one young fellow ... he looks like an Old English sheepdog in need of a haircut ... and do you know what he does on Saturday mornings? He goes round to all the old people, and asks if they've got any odd jobs they want done. And then he does 'em without payment. I said to him once, 'If only you'd cut your curls off, you'd look remarkably like an Englishman.' I'm sorry I ever said it, because he did cut his curls off, and by God you never saw such cauliflower ears."

Like a noble Roman, he accepts with dignity the decline of a nation which he served at its zenith: "The great days have gone," he told the Young Farmers' Club, "and so have a number of very bad ones. If we can manage to prevent the cabin boys from scuttling the ship, we shall remain seaworthy, at any rate in coastal waters." Yet it would be too much to expect that such a man should not feel profoundly sad when he looks back on his own notion of service. Some time ago, while strikers and students were attacking the police, he confessed to his wife: "It's a damned good time to die in." Next day, however, he was planting a copse for the benefit of his grandchildren.

The Commander complains that officers in peacetime are regarded as dragons: "But as soon as the real Dragon comes too close, we're expected to play the role of St George." There is much in what he says, for some people so resent authority (unless it happens to advance their own self-interest) that they revile all who have been trained to wield it, and especially any naval or military officer. Only when their imbecility has imperilled their survival will they accept discipline; and having been rescued by it, they revert to their former folly. How different was the attitude of Steele, who reported a conversation between a Quaker and an Army officer: "When two such as thee and I meet," declared the Quaker, "thou shouldst rejoice to see my peaceable demeanour, and I should be grateful to see thy strength and ability to protect me in it."

Hare and Hounds

The Chiltern hermit always greets me warmly. Neither age nor celibacy has lessened his love of mankind. Indeed, he dwells alone rather from necessity than choice. Our own encounters nowadays are rare, for we no longer live near to each other, but are separated by two hundred miles. The latest reunion took place at a meet of the beagles, which my friend attends whenever they hunt within a dozen miles from his cottage. So there he stood—hobnailed, raincoated, rubicund—discussing corn with a ploughman.

Seeing me, he strolled across. "My nephew-in-law drove me over," he explained. "Oi can't run loike wart oi used, but oi still enjoys a toddle. They do say an apple a day keeps the doctor away. Well, thart may be. But in these toimes it's a soight cheaper to go beagling twoice a month."

We surveyed the field, which was an agreeably mixed bag of farmers, farmhands, stockbrokers, shopkeepers, lawyers, house-wives, children, and a squire's daughter (known to my friend as

"The Hon" or Honourable), whose blonde hair could not quite conceal the fact that she would never see fifty again. In the background stood four shaggy apparitions, carrying a placard which stated *Ban Blood Sports*.

Beagling is altogether less formal than foxhunting. The Master certainly commands, but the nature of the chase makes it inevitable that he should sometimes find himself overtaken by younger followers. The costumes are the reverse of uniform. Some people

wear leggings; others choose plus fours and anklets; others, again, tuck their trousers into gumboots; and a few wear shorts and plimsoles. Liberated women wear whatever seems most likely to emphasise the liberties they have taken, but the Master's wife prefers tweeds and a shooting stick. One north country pack still remembers the two Scottish friars who flouted St Francis by attending a meet. The Master dubbed them "James First and Sixt." During World War II, when a small detachment of Foot Guards were protecting Winston Churchill at Chequers, some of the officers followed the Old Berkeley Beagles, impeccably battle-dressed, with shining boots and razor-creased trousers. After five minutes of muddy furrows, each officer was as spattered and stained as the rest of the field, yet at every meet they were dressed as though for an inspection by their Colonel.

Although foxhunting has amassed a huge literature, from Mr. Jorrocks to *Reynard the Fox*, harehunting attracts little notice. Perhaps the poets dismiss it as pedestrian. Chief among the exceptions was Wilfred Scawen Blunt, that nomadic Sussex squire, who confessed:

> I like the hunting of the hare:
> New sports I hold in scorn.
> I like to be as my fathers were
> In the years ere I was born.

Hunting remains an ineradicable feature of country life, growing more popular, not less. Mankind will need to live many centuries, before it loses the urge to chase. Deprived of that outlet, certain people would treat their family and their fellows in much the same way as a greyhound treats the mechanical hare. Unlike a greyhound, however, they would catch the quarry. If Britain's hooligans went beagling, a great deal of uncivil war might be averted, and most countryfolk would agree that the ends justified the means. Unfortunately, the merest mention of hunting ensures that the mentioner will be reviled as an upper class sadist, for whom hanging is too merciful.

My Chiltern friend, meanwhile, was recalling the years when we trotted up Combe Hill and through the Vale of Aylesbury, less concerned to kill a hare than to maintain touch with the green livery of the beagles. "Reuben came up to me once," he began.

"Reuben?" I asked.

"You remember Reub. He used to keep the Barley Mow."

"Of course."

"Anyway, he asked if we'd killed. 'Stroike me,' oi said, 'oi dunno. Wart's more,' oi said, 'oi don't bloody well care. All oi warnt is a good run and a good gossip and a cup o'tea arterwards. As for the hare,' oi said, 'well, oi 'ope 'ee got away.' " Those sentiments reflect my own so accurately that I cannot better them, unless to add that a hunted hare either escapes or is killed instantly, unlike the one which an erratic marksman condemned to a lingering death.

Dedicated beaglers, of course, pay due attention to the expertise of their pursuit. Thomas Huxley put the matter succinctly: "A physiological peculiarity enables the Beagle to track its prey by scent." First recorded in 1475, the word "beagle" connoted a small hunting dog. Queen Elizabeth I is said to have reared a beagle so small that it could be placed inside her glove (surely an overstatement). But the name undoubtedly became a term of endearment. In *Twelfth Night*, for example, Shakespeare offered it as a compliment to Maria; and King James I called Robert Cecll his "little beagill". William III and George IV each kept a pack, but the beagles were really harriers accompanied by horsemen. Foot beagling originated in Westmorland and Cumberland, where, because of the mountains, the foxhounds are followed on foot. The breed was not officially recognised until 1860, when a Birmingham dog show offered a prize for the best beagle. Fifteen years later the Beagle Club was founded.

Very few farmers forbid the hunt to cross their fields. In return, every Master respects a concession which allows the pack to enter territory that would otherwise be considered private. Even when a beagler can no longer keep up with hounds, he may follow them visually, because a hare tends to run in circles, and from high ground the course can be seen over a considerable distance. Veterans standing on a hill may therefore enjoy a better view than youngsters running through a wood.

All in all, beagling holds its own against any other field sport. It jogs the liver, warms the heart, quickens the eye. Foxhunting may be more hazardous, and shooting more skilful, but beagling combines the zest of a brisk walk with the zeal of a leisurely marathon. At the end of it, Shanks and his pony return home muddy but unbowed, to be rewarded with a hot bath, a high tea, and a deep sleep.

The Gate of the Year

The gate of the year seems never so spruce as when it leads to the gate of the Shires, that well-groomed region northward from Stony Stratford. Northamptonshire justifies its soubriquet, "the county of spires and squires". Many famous ghosts haunt the scene. John Dryden, for example, was born at the rectory of Aldwinkle All Saints; Charles Kingsley lived awhile at the rectory of Barnack; Bishop Percy (he of the *Reliques*) was vicar of Easton Maudit; Robert Catesby hatched his Gunpowder Plot at Ashby St Ledgers; Capability Brown landscaped Castle Ashby, seat of the Comptons; Mary Queen of Scots died at Fotheringhay; and in 1539 the ancestors of George Washington bought the royal manor of Sulgrave.

If you pass through the gate, into Leicestershire, you will over-hear from signposts both a Danish and a Saxon music, mingled with Latin and Norman-French: Goady Marwood, Ab Kettleby, Kirkby Bellairs, Peatling Parva, Isley Walton, Kibworth Beau-champ, Barrow-upon-Soar, Houghton-on-the-Hill, Barton-in-the-Beans. This gateway served as my own introduction to rural England, when, as a small boy living in north Buckinghamshire, I cycled the white and flinty lanes of long ago. Since my father had named Stony Stratford as the northern limit of those explorations, I never mentioned my forays across the border into Northampton-shire. Signposts were less rife than they are now, so that I imagined rather than identified the exact spot—somewhere beyond Lilling-stone Dayrell—where Buckinghamshire met Northamptonshire. I may have been guided by the going itself, for at some places the border was revealed by a change in the surface of the lane. If Northamptonshire spoke slightingly of "Bumping into Bucks", we would retaliate with "Nobbling into Northants". But there cannot have been much difference, because all the minor roads were then a source of profit to people who sold puncture kits.

If you approach the gate from the woodless Fens, or from the wooded Chilterns, you notice first the trim hedgerows, which seem to exist less for the comfort of crops and cattle than for the convenience of hounds and huntsmen. Next, you notice the coverts, many of them planted in order to attract foxes. And after the coverts, you notice the happy hunting ground, the miles of meadows, the acres of arable. Indeed, the Pytchley Hunt is as famous as the Cottesmore, and more truly indigenous because it was founded within Northamptonshire, whereas the Cottesmore came down from Westmorland. It was in 1866 that the Pytchley made their memorable eighteen-mile point of three-and-three-quarter hours. Having returned his pack to Brinxworth kennels at 10 p.m., the Master rode several miles to his dinner in Lamport at 11 p.m., and from Lamport he covered a dozen miles to the Hunt Ball in Market Harborough at midnight. Such were the sagas which prompted Lord Chesterfield to ask whether any man ever hunted *twice*.

If the sun is shining, you notice a number of things that are seen only when winter has scoured the land. Beeches, for example, gleam like satin; and the ground beneath them is paved with copper-coloured leaves. The hilltop trees resemble besoms, each branch a twig. Gerard Manley Hopkins saw those twigs as drumsticks tapping a tabour, and as claws clutching the clouds:

> They touch heaven, tabour on it; how their talons sweep
> The smouldering enormous winter welkin!

Ash saplings resemble candelabra tipped with buds of ebony velvet, most unlike the horse-chestnut, whose buds secrete a sticky varnish, warmly waterproof. Festooned with ivy, an elm might be mistaken for an evergreen. All brooks are either bright blue or burnished steel; and the loam wears a reddish tint, as though it had travelled up from Devon. Seeking the year's first flower, country children soon discover that their search is vain, because yellow gorse will glow throughout the year; violets may bloom for Christmas; and in January the meadows flaunt a daisy, the flower which Chaucer saluted as 'emperice, the floure of floures alle".

The wintry sun is rather a lamp than a stove. With early afternoon it becomes purely ornamental, and at teatime it fades, though not without trace, because it joins the moon in a mutual illumination, so that the flints in the fields mime the stars in the sky, each winking at the other while enacting Tennyson's nightly drama:

> And East and West without a breath
> Mixed their dim lights, like life and death.

One of Galsworthy's country gentlemen could scarcely endure the summer, so intense was his love of the chase. For him the year's gate opened in September, the cubbing season. Most countrymen, however, take a less specialised view of the calendar. They may indeed enjoy hunting, but their ultimate allegiance is with the spring. For them the year's gate takes an unconscionable time to open. They lean on it impatiently, pretending that the snowdrop will bloom next week and that the crocus is eager to unfold. They hope to hear a thrush, a lamb. They finger the buds, as though to warm them on their way. But the pink coats and the spruce winterscape will not be hurried. The snowdrop adds scarcely an inch to its stature; the rosebush, nothing at all. January is both the height and the depth of winter, straining our patience with mist and mud, yet evoking our admiration with snow and ice. And when patience is exhausted, January revives it with a promise which was paraphrased by M. L. Haskins: "I said to the man who stood at the gate of the year, 'Give me a light, that I may tread safely into the unknown.' " Earth's physical light is the sun, which at this season adds a daily minim to the moments wherein the ploughman arrives home before nightfall.

2

Going for a Walk

Every countryman has a favourite walk. It is not necessarily the one which he admires above all others, but rather a route which he follows often, partly because it lies near at hand, and partly because it is neither very long nor very short . . . more, in fact, than three miles, yet less than six. My own accustomed walk begins in the garden whence it climbs to a paddock which I have converted from a wilderness into something nearly recognisable as a meadow with apple trees. From that paddock, by courtesy of a farmer, the way toils to the brow of a steep field, and there I halt, not from lack of breath but from surfeit of beauty, for ahead loom the high peaks of Exmoor. Astern—perhaps thirty miles away— clear weather reveals the high peaks of Dartmoor. No village is visible, because none exists to be seen. The world is ringed by mountains to the south and by hills to the north, with everywhere a switchback of green fields, blue brooks, high woods, bare moor.

At the top of the field I open a gate, and follow a lane until, after three hundred yards, I open another gate into another field and then into another and after that into a third. All the while, on my right, the Exmoor summits advance closer, so that I can count the few white farms on the foothills. Soon the path joins a lane overlooking the tower of my parish church, hidden among trees.

A church, then, and a parish; but no village, no shop, no inn, no garage; nothing at all except a few farms and cottages. We, the parishioners, are protected by the giddiest lanes in Devon, sheer 1-in-3 hairpins, and so narrow withal that every car is mauled by brambles . . . a trivial price to pay for privacy. Few summer visitors challenge the warning sign that is our surest shield, "Very Steep Hill". Of those who do challenge it, most come to some sort of grief; none arrives unscratched; and all vow never to return.

Proceeding through this relic of true civilisation, I pass the church itself, concerning which a guidebook remarks: "High up in an exposed position, commanding beautiful views of Exmoor." A second description is less lyrical and more precise: "Tower (unbuttressed, without W door and pinnacles) and walls are old . . ." One of the Victorian parsons of that church had a grandson, who, since he used to stay at the parsonage, must have followed the way I am going, which is up-lane and thereafter through a gate, following a footpath across three fields, still gazing at the moor on the right, which now looks nearer, higher, wider, wilder. The footpath eventually reaches a lane, opposite the drive to the Old Rectory. I have a picture of the house as it was when the parson's grandson knew it in 1835. Except for an ugly new porch, the place has scarcely changed. I never follow that footpath without thinking of the child and of the priest who helped to indent it, sometimes in the face of a February blizzard, sometimes through an August drought. When the child grew up he wrote a brief account of those journeys with his grandfather: "I behold an old man, with a keen profile, under a parson's shovel hat, riding a tall chestnut horse up the western slope of Exmoor, followed by his little grandson on a shaggy and stuggy pony."

The walk meanwhile continues along a lane which the parson took whenever he rode or drove to his church. It is a highbanked lane, sinuous and without houses, Vehicles *en route* are so rare that you discount the possibility of meeting one . . . until you *do* meet it (a tractor, perhaps), parked at the invisible end of a sharp bend; whereafter wisdom proceeds warily, and is never again caught by complete surprise. At lambing and shearing time you may meet a farmhand, who, if he possessed the gift of tongues, would take the words from Hazlitt's mouth: "What a walk is this to me! I have no need of books or companions—the days, the hours, the thoughts of my youth are at my side."

Having reached some crossroads, the lane becomes narrower, and acquires a grass parting down the middle. Now the moor appears on the left, visible whenever a gate breaks the embankment. For nearly half a mile the lane rises and falls in a straight line, flanked with hills where sheep graze under winter woods gleaming like tufts of black hair. At the end of the straight sector the embankment ceases, revealing the moor again, which changes colour, and may seem to change shape, according as the sun lightens it or as the clouds darken it. In February, of course, the vista is less colourful than it will become when April unfolds the leaves, uplifts the grass, bestirs the birds. Sometimes the vista loses itself in a mist, or half-hides behind a squall of rain. But when visibility remains good, it is enhanced by winter's bareness. Hedges become peep-holes; copses are transparent; solitary trees stand like signposts which a villager can read before the stranger has sighted them.

Presently a Council road sign gives warning of the steep descent. Here, too, grass grows down the middle of the lane, and on it I have planted some primroses by way of greeting to any caller at my house. Over those primroses the beeches merge, forming a barebough avenue. On one side, the land climbs to the brow where, at the start of the walk, I had halted to scan the two moors; on the other side, the land drops away and then swoops up again, carving a deep combe wherein a stream sings throughout the year, and snowdrops cluster so densely that they seem more like flakes than flowers. Suddenly the lane swerves to the right, alert as a diver poised to take the 1-in-3 plunge. At that point I keep straight on, following a tree-lined track which is the drive to the house, an eyrie so hard to find that even an experienced map-reader once overshot the mark, and telephoned to say that he was in a callbox at the nearest village, several miles away.

Perhaps you are puzzled by the parson's grandson. Who was he? Why did I mention him? He was Richard Doddridge Blackmore; and I mentioned him because, having heard the Exmoor legend from his grandfather, he ultimately wove it into *Lorna Doone*.

The Fens

The Fens have outgrown their name. They are no longer a vast swamp, too sour to be sown. On the contrary, they contain some of Britain's richest soil, the famous black peat, yielding bumper crops of corn, roots, and flowers. The Romans drained part of the region by digging dykes, but the Saxons lacked both the wit and the will to continue the work. Not until the seventeenth century did Cornelius Vermuyden, a Dutch engineer, begin his reclamation of Fenland, for which he was knighted by Charles I. Although modern technology has extended Vermuyden's conquest, it has not yet tamed the climate, which at this season may cause even a Fensman to doubt James Thomson's prophecy that March winds and April showers really will bring forth tulips and cabbage and barley:

> Be patient, swains; these cruel-seeming winds
> Blow not in vain.

I spent part of my childhood near Crowland, where you can gaze into space without seeing a tree, or a house, or a hill. One night in 1917, when my father was on leave from France, the pony and trap failed to meet us at the station, so we faced a walk of several miles, along a road that was as icy as the nave of a ruined cathedral. My legs being shorter than they are now, I travelled most of the way on my father's shoulder. I can still hear the clink of his spurs, and smell the scent of the beans, and hear an east wind whining over the dyke. Fenland's air is fresh indeed, but not therefore winsome to cheeks that were nurtured in a more temperate zone. When Celia Fiennes entered Ely, three centuries ago, she remarked: "The Bishop does not care to stay long in this place not being for his health . . ." She observed also the way in which a flat landscape deceives the eye: "All this while the Minster is in ones view at a mile distant you would think, but to go to it is a long 4 miles." Charles Kingsley, who had lived on the edge of the Fens, found in their flatness "a beauty as of the sea, of boundless expanse and freedom. Overhead the arch of heaven spreads more ample than elsewhere . . . and that vastness gave, and still gives, such cloudbanks, such sunrises, such sunsets, as can be seen nowhere else within these isles." Acknowledging the fertility of the swamps that had been converted into farmland, Kingsley nevertheless mourned the loss of "the shining meres, the golden reed beds, the countless water-fowl, the strange and gaudy insects, the mystery, the majesty . . . which haunted the deep fens for many a hundred year." The National Trust has preserved a small area at Wicken Fen, where (in Masefield's words) the water-fowl

> Find peace to have their own wild souls;
> In that still lake
> Only the moonrise or the wind controls
> The way they take.

For so long a friend of man, the wind is now rated his enemy. Yet how variously it served him, and how recently he disowned it. "At the time of my boyhood the old windmills were still in regular use . . . This village had two, and many of the surrounding villages had one or more, so that, whatever way one happened to look, the sails of one or other of them could be seen turning merrily in the wind." Those recollections have an antediluvian flavour, yet they were written by a Buckinghamshire carpenter in 1938. Two decades later, in 1957, a book about mills was dedicated "to the last thirty windmillers and millwrights who keep the sails turning. . . ." In the years when every cornmill was driven either by wind or by water, a drought and a prolonged calm might cause hunger. At the beginning of the nineteenth century, for example, the Secretary to the Board of Agriculture cited a Mr Godd of Quiddenham in Norfolk, who owned a steam-driven mill: "It was, in the drought of 1800, of singular use . . . for wind and water having failed in great measure, corn was brought from ten miles distance, to be grounded by this engine."

Acre for acre, Fenland is Britain's most intensively cultivated region. Riding through Cambridgeshire, William Cobbett admired "the beautiful grass, with sheep lying about upon it, as fat as hogs stretched out sleeping in a stye." Many of those pastures have been ploughed in order to grow flowers and vegetables and grain. I remember passing a Lincolnshire farmstead which appeared to be islanded in an ocean of harvest. No road to it was visible, nor any tree which I might have climbed in order to sight a road. Resolving to discover where the road lay, I walked a full mile along a lane encircling the farm. In the end I found a track that did lead to the house. It was hip-high on either side with wheat, and just wide enough for a wagon to pass. The house itself, like most others in Fenland, was not especially handsome. Some of the little towns, however, achieve an air of homely distinction; and Wisbech is undeniably beautiful, with a row of eighteenth-century houses, no two of them alike, lining the South Brink or bank of the River Nene. One of those houses (it has a Renaissance pediment) was the birthplace of Octavia Hill, a local banker's daughter, who —with Sir Robert Hunter and Canon Rawnsley—founded the National Trust. Miss Hill left Wisbech when she was two years old, thereby missing her initiation into the art of skating, a pastime which had immigrated with Vermuyden. One famous Londoner, Samuel Pepys, was enchanted when he went "over the Parke, where I first in my life, it being a great frost, did see people sliding on skeates, which is a very pretty art . . ." My grandfather once told me that in 1875 or thereabouts some skaters undertook to outpace the train between Littleport and Ely. Sure enough, the fastest Fensman won the wager. Wrestling is another Fenland sport, though nowadays declining, like the vernacular: *frorn* or frozen, *gummidge* or scarecrow, *back-us* or kitchen, *docky* or elevenses. A few veterans still believe in witches, and I suspect that some of them still swallow horrible potions as a precaution against broomsticks which go bump in the night.

If a foreign visitor asked to be shown a typical English landscape, no sane man would take him to the Fens. Few even among the English venture there, unless commercially, or *en route* for a holiday region. That relative seclusion is one of Fenland's merits. Myself, I would not choose to live in Fenland, nor to linger there overlong; but I continue to explore it, always with admiration for the fertile soil, the austere scenery, and Kingsley's vivid skyscapes. The remote parts look very much as they did when I sniffed those beans, nearly sixty years ago.

Filling the February Dykes

It was a wild evening, with the light failing, the wind rising, the rain lashing. On the summit of Exmoor, eighteen hundred feet above the sea, a stunted thorn stretched its branches parallel with the ground, each limb quivering like an arthritic hand trying to wave goodbye. Pebbles and leaves flew past—twigs, too, and berries and ferns and moss—all airborne on a gale that echoed Robert Frost's eschatology:

> Oh, never this whelming east wind swells
> But it seems like the sea's return
> To the ancient land where it left the shells
> Before the age of the fern.

Shaggy cattle huddled against a drystone wall while the rain hissed from their rumps, and was sprayed upward whenever a gust lifted the matted forelocks. Lowland cattle could not have endured such a climate, yet those black beasts tossed the wind on their manes. They were heirs of a breed that had been introduced during the nineteenth century, together with several Scottish shepherds for the hill sheep. Great-grandsons of the migrant Scots still ride the moor, tending hardy Cheviots. Meanwhile, the gale gathered fury, filling the February dykes, and sending large

boughs skyhigh like broomsticks in search of a witch. Having twice been struck by them, the cattle shambled to another sector of the wall, alongside three ponies, all tousled in the wind. The ponies were heirs of a breed older than the earliest record of them.

Parts of the moor seldom see a human being, even in summer. During winter they see only a shepherd, and him not often. Astride his pony through rough weather, he wears a tattered hat over his eyes, and a tentlike oilskin which reveals only his boots.

In his wake a Border collie keeps her nose within inches of the pony's tail. If the shepherd does meet a stranger at dusk, he expresses disapproval.

"Up yere a night like this?"

"They told me it's quicker than the lane."

"Quick it may be, but you'm likely to arrive dead."

"Dead?"

"Look at the colour o' that bog. 'Tis a man-eater. 'Twould gobble 'ee up for supper, cap and all. Poor old Tom Gurney got hisself in one o' they, coming home drunk, the night afore he married. Tom were up to his shirt-stud when we found 'en."

"But . . ."

"At the wedding next day, just when the couple were swearing for better and worse, the bridesmaid pointed at Tom, and said, 'Boy, you've done it now.' And then she pointed at the bride, and said, 'But her were damned near a widow afore she did get 'en.' "

At nightfall a gale tends either to wax or to wane. This evening it waned, as though wearied by twelve tempestuous hours. The dome of dark cloud developed a rift, through which three stars shone. Then a second rift appeared, revealing a glimpse of the moon; and after that a third, uncovering part of The Plough. Presently the clouds disintegrated, and became wisps. Constellations assembled themselves piece by piece, as in a jig-saw puzzle. And finally the moon presided, whitening a clump of snowdrops in the combe. Now botanists take care to hide their emotion lest it distort, or even appear to distort, their analysis. Exceptions to that rule are rare and refreshing, as, for instance, when an academic botanist, Dr John Hutchinson, called the snowdrop "this dear little flower". Such language emphasises the extent to which science ignores many aspects of reality. The snowdrop's common name was first recorded in 1664; its classical name is *Galanthus nivalis L*, the snowy member of a specific genus, as defined by Linnaeus. The flower's likeness to a snowflake is caused chiefly by its lack of a calyx or whorl of green sepals; a lack which makes the whiteness appear more conspicuous to insects flying through a dim wood. Even so, the snowdrop does not rely on pollination, but prefers to propagate itself from a bulbous sheaf of tightly-packed leaves, swollen with food. Dorothy Wordsworth combined poetry and precision when she wrote: "the clustering snow-drops put forth their white heads, at first upright, ribbed with green, and like a rosebud when completely opened, hanging their heads downwards, but slowly lengthening their slender stems." Walter de la Mare once set a snowdrop under the microscope of his intellect:

> Now—now, as low I stooped, thought I,
> I will see what this snowdrop *is*;
> So shall I put much argument by,
> And solve a lifetime's mysteries.

But the snowdrop solved nothing. It merely deepened a mystery: "some consciousness we shared".

Do snowdrops grow wild? Botanists still debate the question. Yet there are many places—far from a house or from the known site of a house—where the flowers cover such a wide area that hand-sowing seems unlikely. An insect must have dropped the seed, there to take root and multiply. A colony of snowdrops really does outshine the elements, as Mary Webb noted:

> The northern bank is much more white
> Than frosty grass, for now is snowdrop time.

Some people greet a snowdrop as the year's first flower; others, doubting that the year can claim a first flower, cite shepherd's purse and gorse, which are always in bloom somewhere. Like the first cuckoo, a February snowdrop takes the countryman by surprise, even while he is seeking it. W. H. Davies regarded the flower as a promise; but it is more than that; it is a fulfilment, because the days are lengthening, and Vaughan's wren welcomes the change:

> And now as fresh and chearful as the light
> Thy little heart in early hymns doth sing ...

An Afternoon with Homer

The signpost stood among trees beside a lane in the Oxfordshire Chilterns. On it appeared one word: *Homer*. Now if the word had been Pindar, I would certainly have felt curious, yet I doubt that the name would have led me in search of the place. But Homer! Is there in literature a man more justly famous? Such was Homer's renown that the Greeks called him simply *Ho Poieetees*, The Poet. Moreover, he seems to have arisen perfected and without precedent. Even Shakespeare had Marlowe's "mighty line" by which to steer. But who was Homer's pilot? If it comes to that, who was Homer?

I forgot to answer my own question, so entrancing was the lane itself, which, having plunged into dense woodland, became what the Council classified as *Unfit For Motor Vehicles*. Since the absence of such vehicles is always a blessing, and since I neither needed nor especially desired to reach anywhere in particular, I followed the sylvan path of dalliance. Beeches predominated, as they usually do in the Chilterns, but their olive-green boles were interspersed with grey oaks, and dark holly, and some silver birches. Slanting through the branches, shafts of sunlight looked as round and robust as the pillars in a Norman church; and at its base, where it touched the ground, each shaft lit the perennial carpet of leaves, causing them to shine more brightly than the rest. Somewhere a squirrel squawked, awakening from half-hibernation. I heard him pattering through the undergrowth, and then saw him leaping from bough to bough, like a brown shadow through February sunshine. Somewhere a robin sang; and somewhere else a thrush, Meredith's herald of spring:

> He sings me, out of Winter's throat,
> The young times with the life ahead . . .

Presently the trees on the left parted, to reveal a combe or bottom; but of Homer I saw no sign. Was it a house, or a hill, or a hamlet? If any of those things, had it been baptised by a scholar from Oxford, which lay at no great distance to the north? And, if so baptised, why? Was I, in short, about to uncover some aspect of the Homeric Question that had eluded Gilbert Murray? By way of preparation, and with only one mistake, I recited the principal parts of *oida*, the most irregular verb ever uttered by the Greeks or by anyone else unless the Welsh. I then reminded myself that, in the opinion of some scholars, Homer was not a man at all, but several men, comparable with the committee who had produced the Authorised Version of the Bible. Finally, I recalled Samuel Butler's belief that Homer was neither one man nor many, but a woman, and young at that. My reverie, however, soon ended, for Homer, like Hecuba, could not hold his own against the bleating lambs, the rustling leaves, the pleasant present.

Having climbed leisurely for about half-a-mile, the track passed a stone farmhouse on high ground away to the right. Very still the house seemed, very remote. At first sight I assumed that it was unoccupied; but a smoking chimney revised the false impression, and was itself confirmed by an air of well-kept contentment. So there it stood, in glorious isolation, peering over the trees and beyond them to more trees, more hills, more sky. Now there comes a time in life when a man ought to put away his childish envy of people's homes, especially when other people envy his own; but I doubt that I shall live to attain such wisdom. Therefore I walked up to the house, admiring its garden, sampling its solitude; and after that I went my way, which brought me to a lonely inn on the edge of the wood. Through an open window I overheard a familiar voice. "Well, boy, it's arter one o'clock. Toime oi got bark 'ome and dished up them sardine sandwiches."

My ears had not deceived me, for out came the Chiltern eremite, an old acquaintance of mine, who lived alone in a tumbling-down cottage astride a solitary hill. Speaking the broad patois of his time and place, the veteran greeted me with forthright friendliness: "You still aloive?"

"Yes," I replied, trapped in a platitude.

"Must be more'n a year since oi saw you 'ereabouts. Been past 'Omer?"

"I don't know," I confessed.

"Don't know?" He glanced in the direction of the farmhouse, along the way I had come. "But you must know, 'cause you *'ave*. Thart's wart it's called . . . 'Omer."

Although I seized this opportunity to solve the Homeric Question, the old man could do little more than repeat the name. "'Omer? Oi remember as the vicar knew a fella by thart name. Real pal he must ha' been, 'cause when Mrs Vicar passed-on, the vicar said, 'Oi've been greatly 'elped by 'Omer.' Thart surproised me."

"Why?"

"From wart the vicar said, this pal of 'is warn't no churchgoer. He were a seafaring charp, apparently. Ah, and he near drowned hisself by steering between two hopossite women. Still, if 'Omer really did 'elp the vicar, there must ha' been some good in 'im."

I rephrased my questions, but without success. The eremite was no Graecian. "Oi've lived on these 'ills marn and boy seventy year," he said, "and oi ain't never knowed a Mister 'Omer. There was always the Reades of Ipsden. They owned a lot o'larnd in these parts. And there was a charp from London. Now thart one *did* give 'is cottage a new name. It warn't 'Omer, though. It were French. Mon Riposte. But oi tell you wart. Next toime you git down the village, just you call at Cobbs Cottages."

"Cobbs?"

"Number foive. And then you ask for Perce, 'cause 'ee's lived 'ereabouts since afore the rileway came to Wartlington. Poor fella's deaf, moind, and 'is memory ain't all thart 'ot nowadays, but if there ever was an 'Omer living in them woods, then old Perce Partridge will put you roight."

Alas, not even Perce could do that, nor any of the professional place-namers. So, for all I know, the Chiltern Homer may indeed have been a committee of men, though I doubt that he was ever a giddy girl.

A Rough Ride to Spring

When February meets March the winter becomes distasteful, like a guest who will not go. Throughout half a year—six consecutive months—dust and ashes have been the price we paid for firelight and warmth. Minute by minute and day by day the lengthening nights closed over us, curtailing our open air activities, and sometimes lashing them. Even now, a storm may cause us to draw the curtains at teatime. Not for another twelve weeks will Perthshire and Snowdonia feel free from a threatening blizzard. Townsfolk evade much of that duresse, for they are sheltered against the weather. They walk on stone pavements, under a sky whose stars are dimmed by the shop windows and street lamps which create what Stevenson called "that ugly, blinding glare." Not so the man who lives chiefly out of doors. Come rain, come shine, he ploughs a field, hunts a fox, angles a fish, sells a cow, walks a dog, feeds a flock, drains a dyke, sows a crop. He is open to the elements; and although his lanes are muddy, they are seldom murky, because no artificial stars dim his sky, that weathervane and windgauge and barometer. Motor cars and railway trains travel warmly well-lit; but of what use are such things to people whose home lies at the far end of a long path through a steep wood? Pot-holed on a flooded lane, eight miles north-west of Ottery St Mary, Coleridge anathematised the Devonshire roads:

> Crusted with filth and stuck in mire
> Dull sounds the Bard's bemudded lyre.

Even among the relatively rain-free Fens, Milton pitied old Hobson, the Cambridge carter:

> the ways being foul, twenty to one
> He's stuck there in the slough, and overthrown . . .

Hodge has for centuries served as a countryman's collective nickname; and while he eats his Shrovetide pancake, Hodge himself grows weary of lamplight and fireside, of frost and snow, of wind and rain. When those guests began to arrive, way back in September, he greeted them partly as a novelty and partly as a challenge. Michaelmas, Advent, Christmas, Candlemas; the days became weeks, and were multiplied into months. Hodge watched his stamina wilting while the novelty waned, for one snowstorm goes a very long way, and there are times when even the most dedicated huntsman would hang-up his horn, if only the sun would thaw the frozen furrows. But the last weeks of winter adhere strictly to the book as it was written by Horace Walpole: "The best sun we have is made of Newcastle coal, and I am determined never to reckon upon any other." It is, then, a war of attrition; of darkness versus light; of cold against warmth; of four stuffy walls against a wind on the heath. At the height of that struggle—say, in January—the odds against him will brace a countryman by challenging his fortitude; but in February, when the days grow longer, a spell of spring-like weather may persuade him that he has already won the battle. Then, like a boomerang, winter re-asserts itself, and Hodge feels that he confronts an invincible foe, as it were a phoenix, able to rise from the ashes of its own deception. Moreover, his impatience is aggravated because he knows that the false spring will soon become genuine. He sees snowdrops, bent by the flakes whose whiteness they outshine. He sees crocuses, gleaming like fragile jewels. He sees daffodils, straining to break the sheath that detains them. Tulips are there, waiting to unfurl when at last the pageant does pass by. Lanes are lined with catkins or lambs' tails, and the true lambs bleat for the ewe. Beeches bristle with bronze buds. Rooks re-occupy ancestral homes. Blackbirds sing, as though June had arrived. Village shopkeepers speed the calendar by switching their wares, so that oilskins give way to lawn mowers, and firelighters are replaced by weedkillers.

Marooned with Dr Johnson among Hebridean rain, Boswell declared: "Nothing is more painful to the mind than a state of suspense, especially when it depends upon the weather, concerning which there can be so little calculation." Little indeed, as Thomas Baker discovered when he compiled *Records of the Seasons*, a survey of Wiltshire climate: "1855. The wheat crop was damaged by summer rain" ... "1856. A good crop of wheat" ... "1860. The worst wheat harvest for years" ... "1863. The most abundant harvest since 1834." Neither new science nor old acquaintance can safeguard a countryman against the whims of the weather. Riding his cob on the mountains above Tregaron, a Welsh shepherd—deceived by the smiling dawn—winces while an east wind reminds him of the jerkin he left at home. Having tarred his boat on a mild morning, and launched her into a calm afternoon, a Cornish fisherman puts-back after twenty minutes, saltsoused and waterlogged. At breakfast-time in Morayshire a housewife opens her door to the sun; at teatime she locks it against the gale. Edward Thomas etched an ancient British trait when he wrote of the cottagers who complained because February was "too cold or too warm or too windy or too wet." And a poet of our own time was justified when he exhorted us not to overlook the death of winter by peering for the birth of spring:

> Let the lozenge linger
> Lightly on the palate.

Sometimes the lozenge is sweet, especially in the south-west, which breeds its own brand of February days, when sunlight warms the rocks at Mousehole, and hears the thrush at East Buckland, and softens the smokestacks at Redruth. Even the bleak north-east receives its miniscule of mildness, when St Andrew's blinks at a grey North Sea that burns skyblue; when the buckits or sandshells at John o' Groats are warm to touch; when the Cleveland Hills cradle their first crocus.

Nevertheless, a countryman does weary of winter. Like Thomas Nashe, he waits hopefully for the day when

> The fields breathe sweet, the daisies kiss our feet,
> Young lovers meet, old wives a-sunning sit.

Winter has not yet reached its destination, but it has certainly broken its back, and may for that reason continue to give us a rough ride.

3

The Village Constable

In every sense the scene was ugly. Slag heaps loomed like mountains threatening the cobbled streets of drab houses. Stale taverns dribbled sawdust under the door. Swathes of mist drifted aimlessly, cold as a clammy ghost. Ugliest of all was the colliery itself, with barred gates, silent yards, grimy cage wheel. In the foreground stood a crowd of miners, grey-faced and sullen. They owned no car, no television, no washing machine. But they did possess not quite enough money with which to feed and clothe their families. And there they waited, a band of muscular brothers who with pick and shovel hacked a mean pittance from the bowels of a dangerous earth. They were not plotting to subvert the Constitution. Most of them were not plotting to nationalise the mine. They asked only to be raised above poverty and excessive toil.

Their leader was a stranger who had travelled two hundred miles from East Ham, with orders to incite violence. Under his direction a dozen miners began to batter the gates with pickaxes. At that moment—sedate astride a Sunbeam roadster—the village constable appeared, blue-cloaked, tall-helmeted, silver-whistled. Leaning his bicycle against a wall, he turned to face the crowd, unarmed and alone, for the demonstration had been planned to surprise even the demonstrators. Although he was greeted with abuse, no one moved against the constable, not even when the East Hammer urged them to throw stones. Then reinforcements arrived, and the thin blue line, still heavily outnumbered, linked arms outside the gate. So, in the end, a clash was averted because every miner respected the law by obeying its officers, knowing that the law is the basis of order; that disorder is the basis of bankruptcy; and that no democrat violently defies a government which has been elected by his fellow-citizens.

Things have changed since those hungry 1920s. Not a great while ago millions of Britons saw on their television screens a large mob attacking a few unarmed policemen. They saw the weapons which that mob wielded . . . knives, clubs, iron bars. They saw the mob hold down a constable while he was kicked and beaten. As during the 1920s, the ringleaders included several strangers from afar. But things have indeed changed, because every one of those modern strikers owned a car; many had played Bingo in Barcelona; and all knew that law-breaking *does* pay, by making other people pay, of whom the majority do not belong to, and would scorn to join, a union of uncouth blackmailers.

The village constable nowadays is seldom required to wage such battles, though he may at any moment confront an armed psychopath. At least he is equipped with radio and fast vehicles. In the fight against crime, therefore, only a criminal mourns the passing of the leisurely Sunbeam, the stately cloak, the fatherly, "Now, now lads! Break it up." Except in desperate situations, when a few marksmen carry pistols, the police rely on persuasion. Handcuffs and truncheons are used only against people who demand them. The other night, in a small country town, I watched a young constable arrest three of the nastiest voters who ever participated in the government of Britain. Each was aged nineteen, and all had attacked an elderly publican who refused to serve them after closing time. How that constable coped! No threats, no blows, no handcuffs; just a firm grip in the correct place at the right moment, and, lo, the unholy trinity found themselves in the back seat of a police car. No doubt the magistrate fined them the equivalent of a month's hard boozing.

Laws work badly when they are bent to please hard cases. But the village constable must mind what he says, lest his words are taken down, and used as evidence that he is a Fascist pig or a Freudian sadist. In fact, however, most policemen belong to the enlightened minority who wish to see less prison, more psychiatry, and—in certain cases—prompt application of the sort of deterrent that seldom invites an encore. Using a less formal deterrent, outside the Red Lion on Saturday night, a village constable can sometimes break the offender's morale by pulling his leg. "Now listen, George. If Ted really did call you a bloody liar, then you call him one, too." George complies, not soberly. "That's right," says the constable. "Now, let's see. Number six, isn't it? Only just down the lane. And, Ted, you're number nine. So get back home, both of you, before the old woman does." And each tipsy Ananias helps the other to flee from the wrath to come.

The office of village constable is very ancient. Saxon England called him *contestable*, from the Latin *comes stabuli*, meaning "marshal of the stables". When the Normans adapted the tithing or group of ten men as a new territorial unit, the chief or tithing-man became the local constable, among whose Tudor successors were Dogberry and Verges. The modern policeman's lot is a lonely one. He cannot patronise the pub, as others do. He cannot join this political club nor that religious crusade. He must be all things to all men, yet nothing in particular to anybody. His own wife and children are sometimes out of bounds. And he is perpetually harassed by the Council for Uncivil Liberties, which speaks (and frequently shouts) on behalf of murderers, forgers, bigamists, rapist, robbers; but never on behalf of their victims. Despite those impediments, the village constable maintains an old tradition in new guise. Sometimes astride a bicycle, more often in a car, he still goes the rounds of his beat. Occasionally he makes a rendezvous with a neighbouring colleague, as in the old times. Twice during recent weeks I have seen him on the moonlit moor, flashing his torch over an unoccupied cottage, checking the level of a flooded river, and generally seeking those unobtrusive clues which Sherlock Holmes detected—a broken window, a recent tyre mark, a muffled cough—things that most of us would either not notice or, having seen, would cautiously leave alone.

A policeman's integrity we take for granted, if only because it is not too difficult for a reasonably good man to remain permanently honest. The few black sheep merely emphasise the quality of the rest of the flock. But the policeman's self-restraint in the face of provocation which would send most other people fighting mad ... that is indeed a tribute to the men, to the system, and to those who command it.

Speeding the Plough

At the turn of each furrow the ploughman cried "Hup!" while the horse's head tossed a brassy jingle at the sun. It was a sight that Lilian Bowes-Lyon admired, half-a-century ago:

> The trace horse, watch her move,
> She takes the hill as a ship,
> Figure-head noble,
> Devours the steepening wave.

During the 1930s a crescendo of high-speed husbandry seemed likely to banish every working horse in Britain. It certainly decimated the number of farmhands, and prompted Masefield's question:

> But now, in topsy-turvy now,
> Who tends the beast and drives the plough?

Fortunately, the mechanised crescendo did *not* banish every working horse in Britain. On some farms the horses never have ceased to be employed, and on others they are being reinstated, not in order to supplant, but to assist, machinery. One farmer hereabouts keeps a pair of working horses, partly because he is fond of them, and partly because they fertilize as well as cultivate the land. So, after all, it is still possible to combine business with pleasure and to express affection without affectation.

Our three native breeds of heavy horse are Shire, Clydesdale, Suffolk. The Shire—which may exceed seventeen hands—is the largest and the oldest, having been mentioned in a Statute of Henry VII, at a time when it was called variously the War Horse, the Great Horse, and the Old Black English Horse. Two centuries ago Arthur Young described the breed as "the produce principally of the Shire counties in the heart of England". The first volume of the *Shire Horse Stud Book* recorded 2,381 stallions, reaching back to 1770. The second breed, the Clydesdales, came from the valley of the Clyde in Scotland. Brown is their commonest colour, and grey the rarest. Like the Shire, a Clydesdale has 'feathers' or silky hairs on the back of the legs. To a layman the Clydesdale and the Shire may appear much the same, but nobody could mistake either of them for the third breed, the Suffolk Punch, which is always of a chestnut shade, and has short legs without 'feathers'. So long ago as 1586 Camden's *Britannia* mentioned the breed. Every registered Punch can trace its lineage to a stallion that was foaled in 1768, at the Suffolk village of Ufford, on a farm belonging to a certain Mr Crisp. Never having been formally named, the stallion was called Crisp's Horse. Among less heavy animals, the Cleveland Bay, a Yorkshire breed, is famous as a hunter, a cavalry horse, and a cart horse.

Few Britons nowadays have ever followed the plough behind a horse. I tried it myself, once or twice, when I was a farm pupil. Having seen my first furrow, the farmer offered some advice: "You might do better if you made up your mind which end of the bloody field you really are aiming at." Yet it looked so easy. You simply grasped the reins in your fist, set both hands on the plough, and allowed the horse to do the rest. Alas, even on level ground a horse tends to wander from the straight and narrow furrow; and when a novice jerks the reins, the animal may respond by completing a semi-circle. How does a ploughman control *two* horses, one of which is a raw recruit? The man himself will tell you that a young horse learns from the example of its elder, which answers the helm steadily and with the wisdom of experience. But how does a ploughman steer his team while he watches the depth of the furrow? Constant practice will enable anyone to drive a passably straight course, but only innate skill allows him to steer the length of a field so precisely that every furrow seems to have been plotted with ruler and compass. At Battisford in Suffolk a sector of road, known as Battisford Straight, was laid along a course which had been drawn by the best ploughman in the district. The site of Rome itself, they say, was outlined by a furrow: *sulcus primigenius*.

Plodding ankle-deep against wind and rain, our farming fore-bears were mighty men, and remained so until the twentieth century, when Maurice Hewlett watched a Wiltshire ploughman:

> So then to work, with heavy foot,
> To rouse his horses with a call;
> And slow as they he puts them on't,
> To hale the plow on the stony down
> Thro' marl and flint, thro' stock and root . . .

Yet those plodding peasants would have appeared as miracles of labour-saving ingenuity to the ancient Egyptians who turned the soil with a wooden hoe. Modern ploughs carry a steel mouldboard which lifts the earth and then topples it over. Scholars used to believe that the mouldboard was first devised in Germany, about a thousand years ago, and that the device soon afterwards reached England. The Anglo-Saxons, however, had no word for mould-board, nor has any Anglo-Saxon mouldboard been discovered. That the Saxons did possess a more or less efficient plough, is proven by *Aelfric's Colloquy*, a Latin primer for schoolboys, which mentions both a *culter* or coulter and a *sulhscear* or ploughshare. Tillage has changed since then, though never so swiftly as during the past century. In 1846, for example, Boydell patented a steam tractor, whose wheels laid down and picked up their own iron tracks. In 1858 Fowler designed a stationary steam engine that dragged the plough across a field and back again by means of wire cables on a clip drum. In 1897 the first oil-powered tractor was built. In 1939 there were 50,000 tractors in Britain, yet the majority of small farms kept at least one working horse.

As the team's head-brass flashed out at the turn . . .

Edward Thomas's poem is still practised by hundreds of British ploughmen. At many farms a horse still hauls a cart, or a harrow, or a tedder; on Exmoor and Dartmoor the farmers still go the rounds on horseback, always leisurely, never clumsily. Only under excessive strain does a horse lose its poise. Though the load is heavy, and the going hard, the creature's glossy quarters suggest strength rather than stress. The head is high; the shoulder is willing; the step is sure. And when a spurt does come, either to shift a tree or to breast a hill, the bells quicken their tempo as the harness glints more vividly. There is a deep satisfaction to be had from the wise continuity of laudable customs. Fashion cannot outdate the prowess of man and beast working together in word-less harmony. Watching a horse at the plough, this hasty generation shares the rhythm of unhurried achievement.

Guilden Mordens

"Of all the properties of plants," declared Gilbert White, "none seems more strange than their different periods of flowering." White was discussing the average period of flowering; but plants often defy the calendar, as Dorothy Wordsworth's *Journal* noticed, on 15th October 1800: "Wytheburn looked very wintry, but yet there was a foxglove blossoming by the way." No doubt Miss Wordsworth regarded the glint of autumnal colour as compensation for spring's slow journey northward, which causes the

Cumbrian crocus to unfold while the Cornish daffodil is dying.

By mid-March the West-country lanes are lined with flowers in various stages of development. Rifest of all, the primroses achieve a decor that would tax the artistry of human fingers. Sometimes they grow from the foot of a bank; sometimes on top of a bank, three feet above the heads of passers-by; sometimes in the lane itself, where frost has eroded the surface. West-country primroses

are plumper and more prolific than those in the rest of the kingdom. They can be as wide as florins, and so fertile that one plant will yield a hundred flowers. Daffodils, too, may line the bottom of a ditch, or crown the summit of a wall. In many churchyards they mark the green mound of a pauper's grave, even as Herrick hoped that they would one day salute his own passing:

> In time of life I graced ye with my Verse;
> Do now your flowery honours to my Hearse . . .

Then there are violets, notably the sweet variety, *Viola Odorata*, whose stems creep among the hedgerows. I have seen sweet violets flowering on Ash Wednesday beside the lane to Little Hampden in Buckinghamshire. At the beginning of April they are joined by the blue wood violet and by the white-centred dog violet. I have yet to find a colony of wayside crocuses; but at Lew Trenchard (Sabine Baring-Gould's old home, on the edge of Dartmoor) one crocus grows in a chink of pavement near the church gate. Wordsworth composed three poems to his own favourite flower, the lesser celandine, a member of the buttercup family, which blooms

> Ere a leaf is on the bush
> In the time before the thrush
> Has a thought about her nest.

A lesser celandine ought to have adorned Wordsworth's tombstone at Grasmere, but the sculptor either misunderstood his directions or was a poor botanist, because he carved a greater celandine, a member of the poppy family, which seldom blooms until May, and is taller than its lesser namesake. According to Pliny, the greater celandine's yellow juice was used by swallows to restore the eyesight of their blinded nestlings; whence the flower's name, from the Greek *chelidonion* or swallow. John Wesley's little-known book, *Primitive Physick*, recommends the juice as a homeopathic cure for jaundice, not to be taken internally, but worn as a leaf-plaster inside the shoe.

No countryman underrates the daisy or day's eye, an unwinking optic insofar as it blooms throughout the year, without ever seeming to wither. Shelley called it "The constellated flower that never sets." If the lane passes a perennially damp piece of ground, it may reveal a kingcup or marsh marigold. Like every other plant, the kingcup breathes via all its parts, but is ventilated by air ducts which rescue it from death by drowning. Although the flower soon droops when it has been picked, it may survive transplanting, like the one that I uprooted at the Crook of Lune in what used to be called Westmorland, and then gave to friends, who raised it successfully on moist ground in Sussex. Cowslips are the Old English *cu-slyppe* or, in polite phrase, a slippery patch, deposited by cows. Botanists call it *Primula veris*, the first spring flower (a debatable priority). The finest cowslips I ever saw were on the banks of a Warwickshire railway near Lapworth. They surged in thousands, like a saffron sea. Varying from county to county, some of the old flower-names would have baffled Linnaeus. They certainly surprised Parson Kilvert, a man of the Welsh Marches, who wrote in his diary: "Old James Jones, the sawyer . . . said that ground ivy or Robin-in-the-hedge is called Hay maids in Herefordshire." Among elderly Chiltern folk the greater stitchwort is called shirt-buttons; the marguerite is called horse-daisy; the lady's smock is called milkmaids; and the marsh marigold is called butter-clocks. In Cambridgeshire long ago I met an octogenarian who was picking what he called a "guilden morden", that being the local name for a posy. John Clare set his own March posy to music:

> Here's two or three flowers for my fair one,
> Wood primrose and celandine too;
> I oft look about for a rare one
> To put in a posy for you.

Spring's wayside pageant is not a formal setpiece, a kind of floral firework display, destined to end abruptly. It resembles rather an informal progression, leading to a Maytime climax of bluebells, speedwells, red campions, white stitchworts, and the last sheltered primrose. At this season, therefore, the villagers walk through a public botanical garden so profuse that not even an army of vandals could noticeably deplete the beauty. An enjoyment of flowers is enhanced by a knowledge of botany, which Lord Herbert of Cherbury rated as part of a liberal education: "I conceive it is a fine study," he wrote, "and worthy a gentleman to be a good botanic, so that he knows the nature of all herbs and plants, being our fellow-creatures and made for the use of men."

The botanic, however, cannot rely solely on books; he must be out and about, seeking such flowers "as usually grow by the highway-side, in meadows, by rivers, or in marshes, or in corn-fields, or in dry and mountainous places." I make no claim to be "a good botanic." My place is with those who Canon Andrew Young classified as *Botanicus Pseudo-botanicus*; by which he meant, not a false, but simply an inexpert, lover of flowers.

A jay's plumage looks beautiful indeed, yet the bird himself is destructive. A child's laughter sounds lyrical; and that, too, may be full of guile. Even a placid river can prove lethal. If true innocence does exist on earth, we meet it in the flowers, for their needs are innocuous; their demeanour gives harmless pleasure; and their thoughts—if they have any—lie so far beyond our understanding that not even a cynic presumes to find them guilty.

Farmland or Fairyland?

"Farming," growled the farmer, "is a mug's game."

"In that case," the foreman asked, "why have 'ee spent the past twenty years at it?"

"For the same reason that I shall spend the next twenty years at it . . . because I *am* a mug. And now let's get those blasted sheep rounded up. And after that the bullocks. And after that . . ."

"After that I'll be watching they old stock cars on the telly. Shall 'ee be watching 'em?"

"No I shall not. I'll be writing to the Inland Revenue, the North Devon Water Board, South Molton Seedsmen, Amalgamated Inseminators, Ministry of . . . hey, those damned sheep have broken out!"

And yet, when all's said, the land and the sea are man's native elements. Factories and offices came later, and do not suit him quite so well; a fact that may explain why many townsfolk regard farmland as fairyland, which it is not. Farmland is a place where men and women earn an arduous and precarious livelihood. William Cowper long ago transcribed the troubled tones of country talk that are heard whenever farmers get together:

> One talks of mildew and of frost,
> And one of storms and hail,
> And one of pigs that he has lost
> By maggots in the tail.

Yet some people still regard farming as an idyll, interspersed with lazy summer afternoons and idle fireside nights. That distorted view ignores two facts: first, our roads traverse only a small cross-section of farmland, so that only a small cross-section of the work thereon is visible to travellers; second, no land can be ceaselessly ploughed nor incessantly reaped; without some respite the seeds would never germinate. There are several rural rubrics—sowing, reaping, shearing, dipping—which reveal the land as a hive of human activity; but those bustling occasions are vastly outnumbered by the days when empty acres and unpeopled farmyards really do create an illusion of idleness. How calm the fields look, void of men and machines. How fresh the March winds blow, like an open window when the guests have departed. How stately the woods appear, black as curls above a furrowed brow. How those furrows gleam when the sun touches them; a sight that caught Frank Kendon's eye:

> the rain that darkens the furrow
> Washes its blades to their right and sturdy green . . .

Even the farmers indulge fantasies about themselves and one another. Mixed farms, for instance, envy the sheep farms' apparent leisure. It is true, of course, that flocks do not need to be milked and that hill farmers have fewer hedges to maintain; but a drought will reduce their winter fodder, and snow may bury it for weeks. A dearth of hay and grass can prove disastrous for the hill farmer, who must spend time and money on buying supplies and on moving them across mountainous terrain. Snowbound at twelve hundred feet above the sea, a northern sheep farmer dreams of the lowland dairyman, forgetting that the herd must be milked every day, the riverside meadows drained, the pastures ploughed and harrowed and sown. One such northerner expressed a poor opinion of the Cornish farmer who had won prizes for his vegetables. "Broccoli?" the dalesman grunted. "That's not farming. It's gardening."

We tend to accept farmhouses as a very ancient feature of the countryside, yet an historian rates them as relatively modern. The word 'farmhouse' did not appear until 1598; 'farming' appeared in 1591; 'farmers', in 1672; 'farmyard', in 1748; 'farmstead', in 1807. The mediaeval farmer or *firmarius* was a bailiff, whose master resided at the castle, or in the manor house. The word 'farmhold', meaning what we now call a farmhouse and its fields, did not appear until 1449. Most of the farmers lived either in a village or in a town, because the average mediaeval holding was too small and too scattered to support a house and outbuildings. A prosperous yeoman built a handsome home: witness the fifteenth-century houses at Lavenham in Suffolk, and the sixteenth-century houses at Shipston-on-Stour in Warwickshire. It was not until the seventeenth century that the majority of farmers began to settle among their own fields. Nine-tenths of our farmhouses, therefore, were built after the Restoration. As for the methods and materials of farming, they, too, have changed with the years. More than a century ago Richard Jefferies noted the silent revolution: "the very races of animals have changed or been supplanted . . . The pigs were of a different kind, and the dogs and poultry. If the race of men have not changed they have altered their costume; the smock-frock lingered longest, but even that is going . . ." So ran the slow tide of change, onward from Thomas Tusser and John Fitzherbert to 'Turnip' Townsend and Coke of Holkham.

At the beginning of the twentieth century, agriculture was the largest single employer of labour in Britain; towards the end of that century the number of farmhands had decreased by hundreds of thousands, and continues to dwindle every year, whittled away by machinery and low wages. Having fouled and squandered our farmland for the past two centuries, industry and commerce are beginning to understand that the soil is a source of food, fleece, hides; in a word, of profit. Once upon a time this kingdom grew rich by exporting hardware in order to earn the money wherewith to import food. At the present time, many of our former customers have either learned to make their own hardware or are buying it less expensively from non-British manufacturers. Greed being always selfish and often myopic, the Industrial Revolutionaries did not foresee our present plight, or, if they did see it, muttered: "Après nous le deluge." So what? So the average Briton rejoices whenever a new factory buries an old field. Time, however, is no longer on his side. The deluge has overtaken him; and unless he amends his ways, not even the oil-glutted Arabs will be willing to feed Britain's redundant factory hands.

4

The First Voyage of Spring

"In human life," said Wordsworth, "there are days which are worth whole months." It was on such a day that *Noah's Ark* made the first voyage of spring. Similar days had dawned before, and many followed after, yet that particular day outshines them all, though it occurred long ago. The weather may have helped to imprint the moment on my memory, because a sullen March was succeeded by a vicious April. Week after week an east wind whipped the creek where *Noah's Ark* rocked at her winter anchorage. Daffodils died without ever knowing a whole day's respite from rain or wind. North-facing hedgerows stood as leafless as on New Year's Eve. Every morning broke grey; every afternoon continued grey. People began to forget what a blue sky looked like, until they caught a brief glimpse of it between clouds. So passed March and the first week of April.

One morning, just before seven o'clock, I awoke to find something moving above the locker seat; something that ought to have been a daily occurrence, but was now so unexpected that it caused me to blink. The thing was water, reflected by the sun. And there was another surprise; instead of pitching, the boat lay as steady as a rock. I went on deck, and for several moments could scarcely believe what I saw. The whole sky was blue. The sea also was blue, and in it the sun minted golden ripples. Hills above the creek shone greener than baize. A cuckoo called from the sea wall below Frooe Farm, and went on calling, each time answering its own echo. Slowly the truth dawned. Spring had returned at last, burnishing the bole of every tree, gilding each buttercup, polishing the primrose. I returned to the cabin, and at once collected every movable object, setting each piece to dry on deck. I even brought out the oil stove, and cooked my rashers in the sun.

Soon after breakfast an old man and a young child dragged their dinghy to the edge of the creek. The child leaped aboard while his grandfather waded out, pushing the dinghy stern first. Then the greybeard hoisted himself over the side, and away they went, pleasure-cruising in the long-awaited warmth. An hour later I fulfilled Walt Whitman's landbound ambition:

> O to sail a ship!
> To leave the tiresome sameness of the streets . . .

Up came the anchor, down went the helm, and the boat moved forward, propelled at five knots by an ancient engine and one square yard of canvas, rigged jury-fashion above the rudder. Among moored yachts we went, past waterside trees, beyond the harbour and the lighthouse, on to the open sea, which had lost its white-lipped snarl, and was heaving gently, like a blue banner on a mild breeze. *Noah's Ark*, a converted lifeboat, rode the swell with zest, eager as a horse that after long confinement has found the freedom of the fields. Seagulls hovered and glided and sometimes swooped. Their whiteness was dazzling; their flight, a miracle of mastery. They serenaded the sea, and with their wings embellished it. Spring had returned indeed, late but not less lovely. Waves, wind, motion . . . all now were gentle and benevolent. The brine was a masculine perfume; the breeze, a blown kiss. So, we held our course, eastward into sunlight, until a deep trough sent the spray scudding across the cabin roof, warning us not to venture too far too soon.

The First Voyage of Spring

How handsome the land looked when we turned toward it. Cornwall curved like an emerald rampart from Portscatho to the Lizard. Helford River was a fairway through Arcady. St Mawes might have been a Mediterranean village, its coloured cottages trickling from hilltop to quayside. At St Just a shirt-sleeved fisherman mended his lobster pots. Percuil was a haven of steep meadows above a sinuous creek. Too distant to be heard, a plough crawled up the slopes of St Anthony-in-Roseland; and there also the gulls had gathered, scavenging each new-turned furrow. Three white sails appeared, and then a yellow; all summoned at the sun's behest.

Beyond Percuil the creek narrowed, losing itself among hills that clustered like green apples on a willow-pattern plate. Having proceeded as far as the fathoms allowed, I dropped anchor, and leaned against the wheel, watching the seaweed gliding by. The wheel itself was warm to touch. The boat's brightwork gleamed as in an advertisement for metal polish. From somewhere across the water a voice shouted: "Spring's arrived at last, eh?" Another voice replied: "Too true, midear. If this weather holds we'm planning to caulk th'old ketch. Her's been leaking terrible since they gales. Coming back from Mevagissey last night we was pumping out most of the English Channel." Taking the hint, I began to pump *Noah's Ark*, ridding her of several weeks' sousing. The first few gallons were an ugly concoction of oil, tar, rain, spray, and sawdust. When the bilges were dry I removed part of the deck, allowing the sun and wind to get to work. That done, I basked in the unaccustomed warmth, hearing blackbirds and cuckoos, and a quiet tide lapping the clinker hull. Fifty yards away some sheep bleated; half-a-mile astern the Customs launch throbbed; at Falmouth a tanker's siren boomed; and the sun, having reached its zenith, ended the Forenoon Watch.

On slack water I returned downstream, not to the winter anchorage, but to a sandy cove under the lee of the lighthouse, where the sea was so clear that I could identify a rusty anchor lying on the bottom. Two people were swimming inshore, watched by two others who were browning themselves on the beach. The breeze had died away now, and a slight swell lifted the boat leisurely, very restful after days of violent pitching. Touched by the sun, the lighthouse windows winked. Was this the same world as yesterday, when I had worn an oilskin against the hail? It was indeed the same world, but transfigured by the light of spring, concerning which there is nothing new to be said, because there is nothing new to be felt. When April waves its wand, man's wonder arises from depths that are older than the pride of his intellect and the *naïveté* of his worldliness.

A New Broom

There was much discussion and apprehension when the Earl announced that taxation had at last evicted him from his home. One of the younger estate workers couldn't (as he put it) care less: "What's the old bastard ever done, anyway? Sweet nothing, except sit on his arse and collect the rent." Older villagers were more intelligent: "And how much is *your* rent?"

"Well . . ."

"I'll tell you how much. It's much less than what it cost his lordship to keep the house in good repair. That's one of the reasons why he's leaving. So talk sense, boy. Ah, and you might start asking who'll employ you when he does go. The Council? The Coal Board? Try touching *them* for a fiver to tide you over your Bingo losses."

Six weeks later the new owner's Rolls-Royce passed through the lodge gates; and five minutes after that the chauffeur was taking tea with the Earl's gardener-cum-butler-cum-groom. As a result, the groom-cum-butler-cum-gardener was able to inform the George and Dragon: "The new chap's called Sir Frederick."

"Oh? What was he Fredded for?"

"Making money. I only wish his lordship could have made some. But he hadn't got the capital."

On the following Thursday, Sir Fred summoned every tenant to a meeting in the ballroom, from which they came away despondent.

"I'm due to retire at Christmas," said one, "so I spoke my mind. 'This is a farm,' I told him, 'not a factory.' "

"What did he say to that?"

"He said a farm *is* a factory. 'What's more,' he said, 'there's at least a dozen men here who are getting paid for doing damn all.' "

"Just as I feared. You and me will soon be asking the nation for assistance."

By the end of the month, however, when only three of the redundant dozen had been dismissed, gloom gave way to astonishment, for every yard of decrepit fencing was repaired and painted white, as also were the lodge and the stables. Monstrous new machines appeared, in barns that had been renovated and electrified. Gates were mended, hedges were trimmed, tracks were metalled. Strangers appeared, brandishing tape measures and theodolites. The agent acquired a new car and a harassed expression.

All those things occurred six months ago, and now the neighbourhood is revising its first impressions of Sir Fred, even although he appears only briefly, and only at weekends. Time will show whether a plutocrat, who regards his estate as a profitable amusement, can eclipse an aristocrat, who tended it as a trust, who knew his tenants by name, and was acquainted with many of their domestic problems, which he eased insofar as a dwindling income allowed. Older folk find the new broom too busy. "He told me to see the bailiff about it. Said he was pressed for time. Not like the old days. The Earl would always stop for a chat. 'George,' he said to me, 'my memory won't keep pace with all your grand-children. I can remember the grands,' he said, 'but when it comes to the greats I get as far as Harthur and Heedith, and after than I'm stumped.' It's different with Fred. He don't even know whether you're married to your missus. Ah, he don't bloody well care, neither."

It is interesting to observe Sir Fred's impact on the lower strata of rural society, which are flustered by his title, but unimpressed by his presence. The uppermost stratum is correct rather than cordial; and, of course, there remain one or two entrées that are not for sale. Some people affect to find no significant difference between a don and a dustman. Simply by being born, they say, every man becomes the equal of all men. But that denies the facts of life, for all men are born unequal; even their fingerprints differ, which helps the police to catch certain egalitarians who rate themselves superior to persons who work for their living. Equality before the law is not at all the same as equality before a selection board. So far, I have met Sir Fred only twice and briefly. At each meeting he struck me as being curt. His country tweeds would seem more convincing were they less correct. Of his courage, however, there can be no question. After only two riding lessons (which took place privately in London) he ventured onto the hunting field, and was thrice thrown; each time remounting despite the pain. Nevertheless, he neither looks nor feels at home in the country. He is a financier, a townsman. His true habitat is London, and he half-regrets having bought an estate so far from Threadneedle Street. "Sussex," he once confessed, "or Kent . . . that's what I really wanted. Somewhere about an hour from Charing Cross." Of course, he lives under the shadow of an old disadvantage. Six centuries ago William Langland complained that "soapmakers and their sons for silver are made knights." Less than two centuries ago William Cobbett complained that the ancient nobility and gentry had been largely ousted by "a race of merchants and manufacturers and bankers and loan-jobbers and contractors . . ." Those sentiments may have sounded proper in an age of chivalry, but they have become outdated in an age of Sir Goalkeeper and Lord Wage-Claim. Hearsay has it that Sir Fred first reached England with one suitcase and a middle-European passport. He may have done; yet his voice suggests that he was bred in Lancashire. To me he seems a lonely figure, a childless widower, whose next-of-kin is a nephew, serving as a Sapper overseas. However, one or two straws on the wind—a remark by the bailiff, an aside from the housekeeper—reveal that the new broom-sweeping is not unilateral. For example, on Christmas morning Sir Fred attended church; he countermanded his own order to cover part of the farmyard cobbles with concrete; he allowed his stockman to override the vet; he withdrew an application to divert the footpath through Manor Meadow; and he granted reprieves to three veteran shire horses. In short, the old estate has already influenced its new owner. When the occasion offers, I hope to form a more precise opinion of Sir Fred, bearing in mind that his breed (the Earl called them "these new chaps") are symbols of change, without which we would long since have joined the dodo.

Water under the Bridge

The bridge crosses the stream at a junction of two combes which are so steep that you must tilt your head in order to scan their summits. The stream itself flows between wooded heights and thence under the bridge, among cliff-like meadows. The middle of the stream marks a parish boundary; and beyond it, astride the brow of a hill, stands one of the two parish churches, lofty as a peel tower set against the sky. Neither parish contains a shop nor an inn, for each is a scattering of farms and cottages rather than a village. Nowadays the two parishes are good neighbours, though in the past they viewed each other less amicably, such was our forefathers' hostility towards all who dwelt beyond the clan. Indeed, the word "rival" comes from the Latin *rivalis*, meaning anyone who lives on the opposite side of the river. One thinks of the bridge across the Lugg at Presteigne, dividing England from Wales, and of the bridge across the Tweed at Coldstream, dividing England from Scotland. Dark were the scowls, and bloody the blows, that passed across those national frontiers.

The bridge in the combe is an old, but not yet an ancient, monument. Single-arched, and just wide enough for a wagon to pass, it was built of stone from the hill nearby. Local people never exceed fifteen miles an hour when crossing, but strangers often exceed twenty, which is why part of the bridge wears an unweathered look, having been repaired a few years ago, after an 'accident'. Like a five-barred gate, the height of the parapet is

well-suited to persons with a leaning towards meditation and the habit of casting straws onto the water, to calculate the rate of knots. A pair of cottages overlook the bridge, and a farmhouse stands within two hundred yards of it. One of the cottagers has planted flowers and shrubs beside the stream, so that in April the banks are bright with daffodils, primroses, violets, celandines. Sometimes you can rest on the bridge for a whole morning without seeing a soul. At other times you may find as many as five people assembled there, from the farm and the cottages. During a drought the number may increase to seven, because the whole of one parish draws its water from springs, and the level of the stream is therefore a matter of domestic urgency. In dry weather the stream sinks so low that it makes the bridge look gawkish, like a swan exposing its legs. Masonry that ought to lie below the surface, perennially dark and damp, shines in the sun, its green moss warm to touch. The bankside grass turns brown while water passes under the arch with scarcely a sound. Twice during recent summers several households became waterless. "Run bone dry, midear. In fact, I said to Charlie, only last night, 'If we don't soon get a drop o' rain,' I said, 'we'll be washing ourselves in cider.' " Such households assess water at its true worth, as a precious commodity. Given enough of it to drink, a hale person can go foodless for a month; without it he will die within four days; in very hot climates, within one day. George Herbert quoted a proverb that was old three centuries ago: "We never know the worth of water till the well is dry." But older than that was Cicero's warning: "*Fontes ipsi sitiunt*," "The springs themselves are thirsty."

After heavy rain the scene at the bridge changes dramatically. The spate surges in tawny torrents, sweeping aside large stones, tossing straws in the air and then catching them again, swirling each piece as though it were a miniature caber. Flowers on the banks disappear, lost beneath the flood. Whenever it meets an obstacle—a boulder or a fallen tree—the stream raises its voice, and swerves like a scrum-half seeking an opening. Higher and higher the water creeps, darkening the bridge's stonework. Meadows beside the stream resemble lakes. Sometimes a lamb ventures too near, and is found next day, impaled against a bough. Then the once-parched parishioners change their tune. "Poor old Granny Gurney said 'tis pouring under the kitchen door'. Her always was the first to catch 'en. Lord knows why they built the place so near the river. We'm lucky, up where we are. But I don't give Granny's kitchen no more than another hour, not if it keeps on like this."

Throughout mediaeval England, when fords abounded, the Church commended bridge-building as a way to salvation. In 1228 the Archbishop of York granted indulgence to everyone who subscribed to erect a bridge across the River Wharfe at Otley. Several of our mediaeval bridges carried a chapel, as at St Ives in Huntingdonshire and at Bradford-on-Avon in Wiltshire. While crossing the bridge over the Calder at Wakefield in Yorkshire, John Leland admired "the right goodley chapel of Our Lady", a fourteenth-century building, endowed with "ten pounds per annum . . . settled on William Kaye and William Butt and their successors for ever to perform Divine service." At Crowland in Lincolnshire the monks built a triangular bridge over the confluence of the Welland and the Nene. In Worcestershire, on Eckington's sixteenth-century bridge, Quiller-Couch detected the grooves that had been

> Worn in the sandstone parapet hour by hour
> By labouring bargemen where they shifted ropes.

Not every mediaeval bridge afforded a dry crossing. Riding through Cambridgeshire, Celia Fiennes reached a "bridge over a deep place of the river under which the boats and barges went, and this bridge was in the water, one must pass thro' water to it . . . but I rather chose to ride round and ferry over in a boate (2 pence a horse) . . ."

In the combe, meanwhile, business continues as usual. Hens free-range through the farmyard, strutting and clucking and pecking. Edward, the veteran Jack-of-all-crafts, whets his scythe, ready to clear a tangle of coarse grass. Farmer Seymour and his horses are ploughing part of a field below Mount Whistle, a hilltop house, hidden behind a wood. The trees remain rooted in winter, spikey and leafless. The grass lacks the lustre that will glow when April has sunned and showered it. At first glance, therefore, the month might be December . . . until you notice those flowers beside the bridge, shining like blue and yellow jewels. And, of course, the birds are loud, filling the air with calls which to men sound like songs, though among the singers they may express rivalry with any bird living on the opposite side of the river. In short, the year begins to flow apace. Winter's slack water will soon become a tide, for tomorrow is Palm Sunday, the season of greening hawthorn, clamorous cuckoos, rising wheat.

News of the World

"Every man," wrote Arnold Bennett, "ought to know the history of his own parish." Bennett was born at a time when many countryfolk spent their whole life in the same house, and seldom ventured beyond their native county. They recognised the parish boundaries. They remembered grandfatherly tales of vagrants who, being parochial responsibilities, were sometimes chased into a more responsible parish. Bennett, therefore, was not preaching a doctrine of perfection when he exhorted villagers to acquaint themselves with the history of their church, manor, mill, alms-house, and such characters as old Tom Tuckaway, who was hanged as a highwayman, yet lived for half a century after the execution, the rope having snapped before his neck could do likewise.

Many people fear that the spirit or genius of the countryside will pass unrecorded because fewer and fewer villagers care to take note of such things. I doubt it. How *could* the spirit pass unrecorded while our local newspapers prosper and abound? Some of those newspapers are provincial rather than local. Others seem scarcely more than news sheets, addressed to a few thousand readers. Yet each one records the pulse of rural Britain. From time to time I keep abreast of events by reading *John o' Groat's Journal* and the *Falmouth Packet*. The latter—which was founded during the eighteenth century—scooped several "exclusive stories" from incoming packet boats. Another rustic veteran is the *Westmorland Gazette*, one of whose editors was Thomas de Quincey. Lakeland, alas, did not long enjoy de Quincey's architectural syntax. A difference of opinion arose between proprietor and editor, not unconnected with the latter's fondness for announcing at great length the discovery of a Celtic Stone Circle or of a poetic manuscript . . . interesting items, but of no immediate concern among farmers who wished to learn the current price of beef. At their best, our rural newspapers publish the kind of information which, like wine, grows more valuable with age. Historians of village life still consult Joseph Ashby's articles in Victorian issues of the *Banbury Guardian*, *Warwick Advertiser*, and *Leamington Chronicle*. When some of those articles were published as a book, J. W. Robertson described them as "the best piece of village history since . . . the Hammonds' *Village Labourer*." A classic of twentieth-century topography, Crossing's *Guide to Dartmoor*, was based on a series of articles which he wrote for several West-country newspapers, including the *Mid-Devon and Newton Times*, *Devon Evening Express*, *Western Morning News*.

Few readers find comfort in the headlines of national newspapers. As Dr Johnson observed, such news is usually bad news: "almost all remarkable events have evil for their basis, and are either miseries incurred or miseries escaped." Local editors, by contrast, seldom harass their readers with universally sombre tidings. The disasters are for the most part homespun, seldom ranging beyond a village burglary, a crossroads car crash, a chapel suicide, a manorial divorce. The crimes and follies of mankind tend to diminish as they approach green fields, so that American politics and Russian imperialism give place to "Former Mayor Had No Rear Light" and "Dorset Woman Denies Stealing Deaf Aid." Townsfolk visiting the country are surprised to discover that, so far from being overawed by London, a cottager pities the metropolitans who have never heard of Tidmarsh-juxta-Twittering nor of Nant-y-eglwys. "We'd a visitor in the village last week, bach. English he was. Said he'd travelled all over the world. 'In that case,' I told him, 'how come you need to ask the way to Llanfihangel Glyn Myfyr?' " Such staunch stay-at-homes like to read about the oldest bellringer, the latest baptism, the largest legacy. The contents of their local newspaper have not greatly changed since George Crabbe described them:

> Promotion's ladder who goes up and down;
> Who wed, or who seduced, amuse the town;
> What new-born heir has made his father blest;
> What heir exults, his father now at rest . . .

National newspapers quiz the world, but local newspapers scan a narrower horizon. Fleet Street cannot be the nation's watchdog and at the same time stand guard over Nether Dollop and Little Quagmire. Those homelier tasks are the privilege and obligation of rural editors. The 'developer' who wishes to raze a Tudor mansion in order to build a Bingo Precinct, the Narrow Bend that causes motorists to cause accidents, the campaign to preserve a Saxon church, sites for toilets, accommodation for tourists, charges for car parks, projects for coastal paths . . . our local newspapers state the facts and then express the opinions of all parties. Many an editor, writing from a small country town, has redressed wrongs which *per se* would have been rated as too trivial for the pages of a national newspaper. Nor may we overlook those aesthetic merits which Charles Lamb cited when he said that the files of some newspapers contain "the first callow flights in authorship of several established names in literature." Richard Jefferies, for example, served as a reporter on a Wiltshire newspaper, to which he contributed many technical articles on farming, and several essays that became classics of rural observation. Dickens sharpened his quill by writing despatches while a midnight chaise bumped him over narrow lanes in remote country. Edward Thomas's poetry and prose appeared in local newspapers and little-known magazines. John Masefield wrote for a Lancashire editor. Such men confirm the words of an eminent historian, the Hon. Sir John Fortescue, who maintained: "There is plenty of space for a literary masterpiece in a column of a daily newspaper . . . let the writer remember that he has in trust . . . the purity, dignity, and beauty of English prose."

Most readers, however, turn first to the local news, the whist drives, beauty queens, centenarians, births, deaths, marriages, markets. If you seek a true register of country life, glance at the headlines in a country newspaper: "Banffshire Goalkeeper Tipped as Councillor" . . . "Bench Warns Sexton's Alsatian" . . . "East Molton Methodists Reject Union With Rome" . . . "Missenden Buddhist Foils Burglar".

Special Occasions

Entering a north country village not long ago, I was surprised to see three housewives scrubbing their doorsteps so early in the morning. My surprise increased when several children appeared, scouring the street for scraps of paper. Finally, I noticed a maidservant polishing the doctor's brass nameplate. Unable to account for this activity, I consulted the postman, who informed me that the Queen was coming. Feeling more than ever puzzled, that the Queen had chosen to honour such a remote and unremarkable place, I enquired the reason for her visit.

"She's not exactly visiting," the postman explained. "She's just passing through."

"When?"

"We don't quite know. According to the radio, she's due about midday. Anyhow, we're definitely on the route."

I thanked the postman, and continued my journey, still observing the general bustle . . . a man repainting his garden gate; another, dragging his dustbin out of sight; a third, weeding his windowbox. So there it was, a community of countryfolk, sweeping and scrubbing because, for a few seconds, the Queen might gaze from the window of her car, approving the spruce village. How different, I thought, were the minority who grudge the small subsidies which go some way towards defraying the cost of Royalty's arduous and perpetual duties.

The villagers of Britain regard the Queen with personal affection and corporate loyalty. Few of them, admittedly, could name either the sovereigns or the dynasties since 1066, yet all are aware that, despite an infusion of foreign genes, the Queen is indeed a Briton. One of her ancestors was King of Scotland before he became King of England. The Queen's mother is a daughter of the fourteenth Earl of Strathmore, laird of Glamis Castle. The Queen's eldest son is Prince of Wales *de facto* by conquest and *de jure* by descent via a Welsh squire, Tudur ap Goronwy, from Edynfed Fychan, who in 1215 became seneschal to Llywelyn the Great, Prince of Gwynedd. This family tree unites the nations in which it is rooted. I remember walking one evening through a Highland glen, where a crofter was unfurling the Union Jack from his roof. I hailed him, and asked what the flag signified. His reply shamed my own forgetfulness: "Tomorrow," he said, "is Her Marjesty's bairthday."

Countrymen feel an especial affinity with the Royal Family's love of horses, dogs, field sports, and the land itself. Sailors remember that the Prince of Wales, his father, his grandfather, and his great-grandfather were professional naval officers, and that two of them distinguished themselves in action against the enemy. There are times when the Scots seem to achieve the closest affinity, as when the kilted heirs of the Stuarts move informally about Balmoral, their Aberdeenshire home. At other times one feels that no loyalty excels London's. The meaner the street, the warmer the welcome, or so it would seem. This cordiality is due partly to the fact that the sovereign transcends politics, and can therefore unite political adversaries. Only a handful of psycopaths prefer sectional strife to national amity. The rest hold the sovereign in many sorts of high esteem. Caernarvonshire, for example, may express an aesthetic allegiance: "Lovely she is. And how smart! You couldn't buy those clothes not even in Bangor." Buckinghamshire may issue a self-denying ordinance: "Oi wouldn't 'ave 'er job, not for all the tea in Choina." Devonshire may admire the royal remembrance of anniversaries: "And the first one he opened was a telegram from Buckingham Palace, saying 'Many happy returns, midear, 'cause today you'm an 'undred." Yorkshire may approve the monarch's non-political role: "In America thee mun vote for a tub-thumper on't owd telly." Only the last of those propositions can be accepted as an argument in favour of monarchy, yet together they confirm that monarchy itself suits our temperament, enshrines our past, and keeps pace with our present.

Although Britain long ago discarded the theory of Divine Right, some of the older cottagers still look upon the Queen as a divinity, hedged about with numinous omnipotence. They incline to believe that the Royal Touch is more effective (and also less expensive) than what they call the Free Health Scheme. Such simple souls suppose that, in bowing to the Queen, we merely salute one person; but the truth is otherwise, for the Queen is the one person through whom we can salute all our fellowcountry-men. Certainly we acknowledge her charm and integrity. Certainly we note the example which her private life offers to families who value the unfashionable virtues. But above all, we perceive that she symbolises the individual importance of every one of her loyal subjects throughout the world. That is what Pitt meant when he told the Lords: "There is something behind the Throne greater than the King himself." Lacking a Throne, many nations lack also a leader who stands above the *Sturm und Drang* of party politicians playing to a gullible gallery.

Certain of our new statesmen dismiss loyal demonstrations as a naïve expression of outmoded emotion. They hope that a single party in one Chamber will eventually achieve a dictatorship of demagogues. They therefore deplore the pride and gratitude with which the people welcome the Queen when she comes among them, not as an aloof tyrant, but as a wife and mother, whose career of public service is so onerous that only a dedicated will-power could endure the burden. Introspection and a pennyworth of psychoanalysis may enable a Briton to sift the outdated tares from the timeless wheat of his allegiance to a benign and impartial parental figure.

The most loyalest toast I ever heard was also the most unconventional. It occurred in Hampshire, and was proposed by a village schoolmaster who had just led his cricket eleven to take tea in the pavilion. Suddenly he caught sight of the Union Jack, flying from a flagpole to mark the Queen's birthday. Teaspoon in hand, he glanced at the assembled villagers. "Gentlemen!" he cried; whereupon the thirsty company looked up, each with a cup on the brink of his lips. "Gentlemen, there are some who would like Parliament to destroy the constitution. To destroy it, if necessary, by means of a single vote, and in defiance of the wishes of the majority. Against such knavish tricks the Crown might lawfully defend us by dissolving Parliament and by holding a general election, so allowing us to return a truly representative House of Commons. That, my friends, is not a legal fiction. It is a constitutional fact. Let us give thanks for it, and let us hope that we shall never need to use it." Then, as though the tea were champagne, he raised his cup: "Gentlemen, the Queen."

5

Serenade for Spring

Year after year the spring returns unchanged, and is greeted with the same old jubilation. Spring, therefore, is one of those experiences—love being another, and sleep a third—which we are content to take as they come; indeed, so content that we can scarcely imagine how to improve them. Chaucer, for instance, hailed the season whose sun and showers nurture "In every holt and heath the tender croppes." Six centuries later, Robert Bridges pointed to the same blue sky:

> Behold! the radiant Spring,
> In splendour decked anew,
> Down from her heaven of blue
> Returns a sunlit way . . .

Vergil knew that the spring never falters: "*Nec requies, quin aut pomis*", "Unfailingly the year lavishes fruit, or lambs, or corn . . ." Two thousand years later, Gordon Bottomley descanted on the same theme:

> His acre brought forth roots last year,
> This year it bears the gleamy grain;
> Next spring shall seedling grass appear;
> Then roots and corn and grass again.

The prophet rejoiced because "the winter is past, the rain is over and gone; the flowers appear on the earth; the time of the singing birds is come . . ." Thousands of years later, Vita Sackville-West bade us beware lest perennial suffering should dim the passing joy:

> Let us forget the sorrows: they are there
> Always, but Spring too seldom there . . .

In the years before they had learned to grow winter keep for their livestocks our fathers eked a dwindling ration of salted meat and fish. Lacking paved roads and windproof houses, they went wet and windy from Michaelmas to Easter; and when at last the sun prevailed, they did not suppress their thankfulness. Neither age nor custom has cloyed the infinite variety of Shakespeare's serenade to a season

> When daisies pied and violets blue,
> And lady-smocks all silver-white,
> And cuckoo-buds of yellow hue,
> Do paint the meadows with delight.

That song was paraphrased in prose, three centuries later, when Francis Kilvert walked a Herefordshire lane: "birds singing," he wrote, "buds bursting, and the spring air full of beauty, life and hope." Even Thomas Hardy, a professional pessimist, allowed that May's light and shade were not wholly distasteful:

> This is the weather the cuckoo likes,
> And so do I . . .

Our literature is loud with the same old news, the identical glad tidings. Izaak Walton asked a question so simple that none can answer it: "How do the Black-bird and Thrassel with their melodious voices bid welcome to the chearful Spring, and in their fixed Months Warble forth such ditties as no art or instrument can reach to?" Gilbert White, a scientific observer, paid his own verifiable tribute to spring: "the thermometer rose to 66 degrees in the shade; many species of insects revived and came forth; some bees swarmed; and the old tortoise at Lewes in Sussex came forth out of its dormitory." Richard Jefferies wove a tapestry of progression: "The green hawthorn buds prophesy on the hedge; the reed pushes up in the moist earth like a spear thrust through a shield; the eggs of the starling are laid in the knot-hole of the polarded elm . . ." Watching the Maytime trees, Eden Phillpotts decided that no sane man could "stand amid their bright column and look upward to the blue that frets their darkness, downward to the azure earth seen afar between their aisles, without tribute of joy and wonder." Travelling behind the lines in war-ravaged France, Edmund Blunden noticed "the fields tilled and young crops greening." To Leigh Hunt even the season's name sounded melic: "What a beautiful word is *Spring!*" And he was right, because the grass does spring up, like the flowers and the corn and the sources of water, until the whole land is filled with "fountains, buds, birds, sweetbriars, and sunbeams". Consider the multiplicities of May: May Queen, May-pole, May-bloom, May-term, May-apple, May-bug, May-bush, May-butter, May-cock, May-drew, Mayflower, May-fly, Maying (a word that was first recorded in 1470, as a synonym for celebrating the Queen of Months).

Not all who watch it can enjoy the spring. There are some for whom life breeds more thorns than roses; others, for whom the season brings sudden anguish, a barbed bolt from the blue. Nevertheless, the healing power of Nature, *vis medicatrix Naturae*, is not an illusion. On the contrary, it is the doctor's surest ally, whether as a tissue repairing itself, or a herb making medicine, or free-association purging unconscious conflict. Only the deepest distress fails to find consolation while bluebells pave a fairway through the wood. Mary Webb stated a fact when she said that the spring, "if men will open their hearts to it, will heal them, will create them anew, physically and spiritually." Nor did she err in setting quality above quantity: "Dawn, seen through a sick woman's window, however narrow, pulses with the same fresh wonder as it does over the whole width of the sea." Thomas Gray was able to scan a wider horizon: "I set out one morning before five o'clock . . . and got to the sea-coast in time enough to be at the sun's levée . . . I shall remember it as long as the sun, or at least as long as I endure." Listening to a cuckoo in Hampshire, Rose Macaulay thought it "the finest merry melodious canticling you can hear . . . " Charles Lamb, who spent nearly forty years on a clerk's stool in London, never forgot those rare occasions when he spent a spring day in the country: "It was," he wrote, "like passing out of Time into Eternity—for it *is* a sort of Eternity for a man to have his Time all to himself."

Despite metalled roads and electric blankets, a modern country-man shares an ancient craving. After seven cold and muddy months, he utters Meredith's thanksgiving:

> But now the North Wind ceases,
> The warm South-west awakes,
> The heavens are out in fleeces,
> The earth's green banner shakes.

Brimstone and Broomsticks

The old man stared at the white paint and the repointed walls. "My, my," he exclaimed, "I don't hardly recognize the place. You've certainly slapped a new look on 'en." Then he quizzed the lawn and flowers which had sprung laboriously from a wilderness of mud, rubble, briars, and many trees stunting one another in their struggle for survival. Still shaking an astonished head, the veteran stared again at the house. "In my young days," he recalled, "this yere was two cottages. Old Norman lived in one, and the Witherbys they lived down there, a foot or two lower. But I see you've had 'em joined." He fingered the new corridor. "This stone is local."

"Very local," I replied. "It came from that fishpond."

"Fishpond? Norman never had no fishpond."

"But I have."

"So I see. 'Twas where he chucked his rubbish."

"It was indeed. Bicycle wheels, medicine bottles, kettles, saucepans . . ."

"Oh aye. He were allus a tidy man, old Norman. Never kept anything if he could throw 'en away."

Our conversation had begun a few moments earlier, when a benign old farmhand tapped on the door. "I hope 'ee don't mind me walking up the drive," he said. "Fact is, I've heard 'ee made some changes latterwhile. My auntie did live yere. Leastways, her lived in one of 'em. Pokey old place it were. No doubt you've a pull-chain these days?"

"And a bath, too."

"Auntie had one o' they. A tin one. But she considered 'twas unhealthy. Her uncle took a bath once, and died half an hour later." The visitor gazed politely at the roof. "I would dearly love to peep inside."

We will pass over the visitor's astonishment, for the two cottages had indeed been primitive and small. They still are small, but no longer unmodernly inconvenient. Five minutes later, while we sipped cider in the garden, the old man remarked on the view from one of the paddocks. "You can't quite see Dunkery . . . that's away to Somerset, anyhow . . . but I've often watched the sheep on the tops above Simonsbath, and up there you'm sixteen hundred feet in the clouds. In clear weather you can see Dartmoor, too. Old Zachary were praper perceptible about Dartmoor. 'If you can seen 'en,' he used to say, 'that means 'tis going to rain. And if you *can't* see 'en, that means 'tis raining already.' "

Just then a tractor droned from the valley. "You'm not even on a lane yere," my guest observed. " 'Tis purty quiet, eh?"

"That's one reason why I like it."

"Old Norman liked a bit o' quiet, too." He pointed at the wood which separates the house from the lane. "When Joe Zachary led his plough team up that lane twice on the same day, old Norman lay in wait for 'en, and then he jumped out and said, 'Zacy, midear, you've been up twice since sunrise, and that's once too often for any man. So leave me in peace, will 'ee!"

The farmhand glanced towards the valley behind the wood. "Who owns Mill House nowadays?" he asked.

"Farmer Zillah," I replied. "A good neighbour."

"When Norman were living yere alone, and getting a bit long in the tooth, I used to say to 'en, 'You'm very neighbourly up yere, Norm. You can't see 'em, and you can't hear 'em, yet there they be, away in the combe. And if you was to fall down dead all of a sudden,' I said, 'you've only to walk a half-mile to Mill House, and they'd be up in no time.' "

"I'll remember that."

"How far to the nearest shop?"

"Several miles."

" 'Twas the same when Auntie lived yere. Her ran out o' candles one day . . . round about Christmas time, I remember . . . so her walked down to Brayford . . . that must be three mile or more . . . and when her'd got halfway, along came a blizzard. Well, Auntie managed to reach Brayford, but her didn't manage to get home again. Three days her were stuck, biding with old Zachary's daughter. Ah, and when her did get home, her'd forgotten to buy they candles. Rum old girl, Auntie. Some folks said her were a witch. There used to be a postman, living beyond Mole's Chamber, and one day he said to me, 'If I weren't a Methody,' he said, 'I'd ask the rector to fumigate your aunt with bell, book, and candle.' Whenever Zachy's sheep got the scab, 'twas allus Auntie who'd mesmerised the drench. And whenever a young woman got herself miscarriaged, 'twas allus Auntie who'd put a spell on 'en."

"Did she put a spell on you?"

"Only once. And even then it didn't stick. I'd a wart on my middle finger, and Auntie said to swallow some brimstone, and fry a mouse, and then rub the grass on 'en. 'Tis wonderful what folks did believe in. Ah, and still do believe, some of 'em. My brother's a thatcher, see, and when he went reeding in Norfolk he met a farmer who'd had his front door made o' holly so's to ward-off evil spirits and all such as go bump in the night."

"There was certainly a great deal of superstition."

"They believed it, though. Folks used to come up yere for a medical recipe. Auntie had plenty o' they. Ah, and they weren't all dud 'uns neither."

"Not?"

"No indeed not. I could name a doctor or two as laughed in her face, but when they came to treat my wife for colic, 'twasn't no latest cure they used. 'Twas Auntie's recipe, though they'd jigged 'en up in fancy language."

The old man leaned forward, like a wizened Puck peering through centuries of pagan Christianity. "There's a party living yereabouts as won't never allow hawthorn blossom in the house. If you was to ask why, her'd tell 'ee 'twas an untidy blossom, always needing a dustpan to sweep 'en away. But that ain't the real reason. 'Tis on account of her believes the blossom can kill people. I know that for a fact, 'cause when her was took ill, her looked out o' the bedroom window one day, and saw a hawthorn in bloom, and begged me to cut 'en down in case it came inside."

He sank his cider, and reached for his stick. "Ah, well. Thank 'ee for letting me peep at Auntie's old place. 'Tain't pokey no more."

On Wheels of Song

Of all modes of private transport cycling is the most arduous and the least dignified, unless the cyclist happens to be a cavalry colonel as upright as the handlebars of his 1920 Sunbeam roadster. I lately acquired a modern version of that vehicle, which cost four times more than the colonel's, and was made of such inferior material that several nuts and bolts rusted within a month.

Nevertheless, the machine looks very like the Sunbeam which I used to own. It has a gearcase, a three-speed gear, and is altogether a vehicle which grown-ups can mount without feeling that they are part of a music-hall act. While riding it, I tend to forget Bernard Shaw's pedestrian mockery: "the most ridiculous sight in the world is a man on a bicycle . . ."

Bicycles, they say, were first introduced to England in 1818, by a Baron von Drais of Mannheim. Nicknamed the 'hobby-horse', the contraption was simply a scooter with an uncomfortable saddle. In 1864 a Frenchman, Pierre Lallement, designed a 'hobby-horse' with front-wheel drive and iron tyres (whence a second soubriquet, 'Boneshaker'). My own thanks go to an obscure man, named Thompson, who in 1848 produced pneumatic tyres. The book trade was swift to exploit an up-and-coming cult. So long ago as 1869 a certain A. Davis wrote *The Velocipede: Its History and Practical Hints How to Use It*. In 1903 the legal profession joined in, or was co-opted, with *Everybody's Cycling Law*. Then came Mammon, with *The Cycle Industry* (1921), and after that the tourist trade, with *Round the World on a Cycle* (1929). Throughout the first half of the twentieth century you often saw a posse of bicycles outside the village pub, or beside the church gate, or at the entrance to the cricket field. Thereafter, however, national insolvency enabled most cottagers to arrive by car.

Since I live near the summit of a hill, and am defended from 'civilisation' by a range of near-mountains, my friends expressed surprise that I had acquired any bicycle at all. "Cycling," they murmured, "is a young person's pastime." There are moments when I agree. One thing is certain; in order to *feel* the steepness of a hill, you must cycle up it. For example, there is in these parts a lane which any car will climb in top gear. Walking there, I scarcely notice the gradient; on horseback, I am aware only of the animal's easy gait; but on a bicycle . . . well, I very soon get *off* a bicycle, pushing it as though it were a perambulator. Even so, to cycle among quiet lanes in level country is both restful and bracing. If you are hale, it is pleasant to cycle through steep country. After all, a short walk not only varies the muscular tension but also enhances the moment when, having remounted, you accelerate from three to twelve miles an hour. Anything above that speed is simply a form of outdoor gymnastics, exhilarating, no doubt, but useless to the man who seeks the sights and sounds of the countryside. Fenland is the cyclist's paradise, at any rate when an east wind does not impede him. Essex likewise can be recommended, together with Northamptonshire, Leicestershire, and that part of Leicestershire which I shall continue to call Rutland. Devonshire, on the other hand, is not a good advertisement for the cycle trade. By comparison, Lakeland seems flat, and Perthshire a range of hillocks. But high hills and adverse winds are no longer the cyclist's chief enemy. His ruthless adversary is the motorist. Only a drunkard, a hero, or a lunatic would nowadays cycle along a main road. In summertime even the quietest lanes are scorched by the tyre marks of speeding vehicles.

Weather and circumstances permitting, winter is the best cycling season, especially when a windless air brings clear visibility and the hint of frost. The next-best season is May, especially when a mild breeze brings white clouds and the scent of blossom. There have recently been several such days hereabouts, and on one of them I cycled along the levellest of our lanes, to the tune of lambs and larks. Now prose has its place in human affairs. Some people use it to write manuals on steam engines; others, to make political speeches. Shakespeare used it, too, and so did Shelley; but when they heard a skyful of larks, or watched a field of lambs, they turned to that other and greater harmony, which the Greeks called 'poetry' or 'creation'. Six white clouds, I noticed, sailed on a deep blue sky. Apple blossom pointed a pink tongue; grass swayed like green silk; and the birds made modern verse sound rather dated. In fact, their song was so lyrical that I ventured to compose one of my own extempore and despite the fashion:

> The world is wearing Sunday-best,
> Each tree and hedgerow gaily dressed
> Alike in green
> Whose rain-rinsed sheen
> Smiles at the sun, and preens itself, as though
> The branches and the buds were belles and beaux.

Presently the lane reached a stream, where I halted, leaning over the bench-marked bridge; and among the reeds I saw my second stanza:

> Blue as a ribbon, rivers lie
> Like miniscules of fallen sky
> Come down to earth
> For spring's rebirth,
> Singing their water music, cool and clear,
> To serenade the sweetheart of the year.

Having crossed the bridge, the lane passed a cottage, whose chintz curtains waved a welcome to the breeze. After that, it came to an inn, whose inmates were outmates, sunning themselves beside the porch. There, too, the birds sang, the sun beamed, the trees shone. At ten miles an hour I could feel the breeze on my face, and still had time to glance over hedgerows and to scan the farmyards.

During the next half-mile I pushed the bicycle uphill through an avenue of elms, and by the time I had scaled the summit, my song was complete:

> Old men on tavern benches sit,
> Quizzing the sun, and sipping it;
> All windows wide,
> Spring steps inside
> —Lavender, lilac, bluebell—to display
> An aromatic rainbow, spanning May.

One of the Old School

He has lately retired with his widowed sister to a village in the Shires. Among his friends he is 'Mr Chips', though you may think that 'Colonel' would be a better nickname, because he carries himself erect, clips his grey moustache, and looks more like a retired soldier than a superannuated schoolmaster (in 1942 he won the D.S.O.). Now, at the age of sixty-six, he is ruddy-cheeked, blue-eyed, and so versatile that his interests embrace carpentry, beekeeping, Greek epigraphy, Samian pottery, Alpine plants, and the relative merits of Steve Fairbairn and Gully Nickalls. On most mornings in May he is to be seen at his rockery, wearing a lovat tweed suit with knickerbockers, as befits an occasional beagler and a perennial walker. His head is shaded by a panama hat with a Leander ribbon, both of which, since he acquired them forty years ago, have lost their original colours.

The hat, in fact, has deepened from off-white to on-brown, and the ribbon has faded from bright pink to something resembling a rice pudding streaked with strawberry jam.

Like an old photograph, Mr Chips reminds you of the extent to which Britain has changed during the past half-century. He refers to the Queen as "Her Majesty," and to most other public figures he accords a proper style, "Mr X", for example, "or Lord Y". Only by way of disapproval does he withhold those courtesies, as when he speaks of "Harold Wilson" and "That fellow Foot". In parliamentary affairs he steers clear of the Left, preferring to hold a course between what he calls the Liberalism of the unenlightened and the Mammonism of the unenlightenable. His political creed was summarised by Thomas Hardy: "Opportunity should be equal for all, but those who will not avail themselves of it should be cared for merely—not to be a burden to, nor the rulers over, those who do avail themselves thereof." Since Mr Chips has no television, and is a selective listener to the Third Programme, his speech remains untainted by jargon; not that he was ever likely to become infected by it, for he took a First in Greats, and spent much of his life correcting the vulgar expression of shallow ideas.

He sometimes amuses himself by correcting the bad grammar of certain documents issued by government departments. Having done so, he returns the documents, in an unstamped envelope on which he writes "OHMS". Unlike almost every other Briton, he pays all his bills within twenty-four hours of receiving them.

Mr Chips's philosophical views may appear modern, but are as old as the Classics which he taught at a public school. Thus, when he and his sister first settled in the village they were visited by the vicar, a young man lately translated from Liverpool, whose clerical collar—if, indeed, he wore one—was hidden beneath a roll-neck sweater. Mr Chips promptly identified himself as a Lucretian, hoping thereby to conduct the interview frankly yet without affront. When it became evident that the vicar knew nothing of Lucretius, Mr Chips explained that, in his opinion, the gods had long ago left this star to its fate. The vicar could not understand why such a cheerful man should hold such a sombre outlook; to which Mr Chips replied, that we ought to be gay while we can, grave when we must, and at all times sceptical, even towards our own scepticism. After the meeting, Mr Chips remarked to his sister: "How *can* an intelligent person really believe that the ultimate truth was revealed once and for all, two thousand years ago, to a semi-barbarous tribe?" On a purely literary level, his love for the language of the Bible comes close to idolatry: "By comparison," he once said, "Henry James sounds like a flabby serpent in search of a full-stop. The fifty-seven men who translated the Authorised Version almost persuade me that I am an Anglican." Yet he remains a Stoic, a Classic. William of Wykeham would nod with envious approval, could he hear Mr Chips declaiming the glory that was Rome: "*Aeneadum genetrix hominum divomque voluptas . . .*"

But Mr Chips incurred a handicap more serious than agnosticism when the local divorcée whispered that all elderly celibates were (as she put it) "queer fish". Now there are many reasons why a person does not marry. Some of them are repellent; others are merely pitiful; one or two are noble. The village ladies believe that Mr Chips was crossed in love, or from some other cause failed to win the only girl whom he did wish to marry. All who know him accept him as proof that many spinsters and bachelors are conspicuously less 'queer' than many husbands and wives. The villagers certainly accept him. Today he is chairman of an education committee; he serves on a hospital board; and, despite Lucretius, he has just helped to launch an appeal to restore the church tower. From time to time he is visited by former pupils and by their children who are also former pupils. Such visitations confirm that he escaped the occupational hazard which Roger Ascham cited: "there is no one thing that hath more either dulled the wits or taken away the will of children from learning than the care they have to satisfy their masters in making of Latins." His own views on education are eclectic. For the majority, he favours Froebel and Pestalozzi; for the elite, Winchester as it was when he fagged there. To those who will one day work on the land, he commends Cobbett's recipe for the education of an unacademic country boy: "he has learned to hunt, and shoot, and fish, and look after cattle and sheep, and to work in the garden, and to feed his dogs, and to go from village to village in the dark."

Like a Roman of the old school, Mr Chips upholds his personal ethos against the fashion that mocks it. Being supple enough to adopt good innovations, he has exchanged an erratic Gold Hunter for a reliable wristwatch; being strong enough to resist bad conventions, he still speaks of "Westmorland", and vows that he never will speak of "kilometres". He supports the Establishment in order that it may improve itself; and his lifelong acquaintance with the thoughts of great men enables him to detect the pretensions of little ones. Temperament and upbringing made him an integrated person. His unbelief is leavened with *pietas*; his humour, with *gravitas*; his dignity, with *charitas*. Farmers like him because he can recognise a good crop of wheat. Children like him because he carries toffee. Shopkeepers like him because he pays cash. And the squire likes him because both of them were Gunners. Confidently yet unobtrusively, Mr Chips has enriched the life of the village, and the village repays him in kind.

6

The Four Faces of Summer

An English summer day is quartered like a shield, each segment blazoning its own sights and sounds; the first quarter and the last being tinctured with sable. All of the quarters are unique, but none can be relished fully unless it is viewed as part of the whole, both a prelude and an aftermath. To some people the dawn seems best; to others, the forenoon prime; to others, again, the ripeness of afternoon; and to a few, the night. In June a countryman can— as Edward Thomas put it—"bite the day to the core".

Day's first quarter has become almost a monopoly of farmfolk and sailors, to whom may be added late sleepers (taximen, revellers, nightwatchmen) and early risers (milkmen, postmen, policemen). Among dawn's devotees the sunrise is as magical as moonlight, and more zestful. Freshness and shyness are the hallmarks of dawn, culminating in a glory of light and a lyric of birdsong which make the gay heart gayer, and to a heavy heart offer Masefield's challenge:

> And we, who had to ride, rode on,
> From Ilion to Avalon,
> To cities promised, from towns gone.

Homer praised the dawn, naming it "rosy-fingered". Shakespeare summarised its call to action:

Night's candles are burnt out, and jocund day
Stands tiptoe on the misty mountain tops.
I must be gone, and live . . .

Many other poets uttered their own paean, but few have excelled
the invitation that was extended by Thomas Bewick, who, as a
Northumbrian, rose with the sun: "I have often thought, that not
one-half of mankind knew anything of the beauty, the serenity,
and the stillness of the summer mornings in the country, nor have
ever witnessed the rising sun's shining upon the new day."

Having lit the scene, and promised warmth, the first quarter
gives way to mature morning. In place of mystery and reticence—
the lightening woods, the reappearing hills—day offers clarity and
confidence. Their chorus spent, the birds come literally down to
earth, foraging food for fledglings. Fine weather or foul, somewhere a wisp of smoke climbs from a chimney. Voices are heard.
Windows are opened. Men go forth to milk and to mow. Women
spank the doormat, as though it were a naughty child. Wise in his
generation, an old farmhand has already done three hours' work,
and lies at ease under a hayrick, sipping tea while the church clock
strikes ten. There is nothing shy now about the sun, nothing
mysterious. The sun dominates the earth, drawing attention to
itself. Village shopkeepers cover their perishable goods. Shirt-
sleeved and slippered, the publican sits in the shade of his flower-
filled hearth. Down by the sea, the waves are warming-up, and the
sands already hot. Inland, the moorland heather shimmers
through a purple haze while snow on Ben Nevis retreats to its
bastion in a shadowy crevice. At noon the land is lit by

The fiery pomps, brave exhalations,
And all the glistening shows o' the seeming world.

Passing its meridian, the sun permeates every crevice, burnishes
each flower, stings all skins. Alone in a field, one elm mimes a
sundial, its shadow advancing slowly like a tide of dark water.
Cattle seek the furthest corner of the coolest shed. Only a chiff-

chaff sings, insistently naming itself from the topmost branch. Buttercups sweat. Foxgloves droop. Lizards bask. Men, however, must work, reaping a field, counting a flock, mending a gate, caulking a ketch, whetting a scythe, loading a wain. Sunburned and satchelled, children scamper out of school, laughing as they leap from pool to pool of sunlight where it dapples a woodland path. Their voices echo down the honeysuckle lanes, and as each child reaches its home, the gate creaks, the dog barks, the door opens. While holidaymakers roast their near-nudity, many of the villagers take tea indoors, sometimes behind drawn curtains, for to them the countryside in June is no novelty, and the sun can seem too much of a good thing. So the day wears on, growing hotter and hotter. At six o'clock it is difficult to remember the scene as it was when the sun surmounted the hill, when the dew glistened, and the bees slept, and the birds sang, and the brook spoke. At seven o'clock a farmhouse casts its silhouette halfway across a field. At eight o'clock the cattle, emerging from the shed, sway towards the river, sedulously swishing their tails in a reflex battle with the flies. At nine o'clock the cottagers talk to neighbours across the lane, or stroll in the cool of the evening, as they did at John Clare's home:

> Just as the even-bell rang, we set out;
> To wander the fields and the meadows about;
> And the first thing we mark'd that was lovely to view,
> Was the sun hung on nothing, just bidding adieu . . .

The end of the last quarter resembles the start of the first, because the glow from the sun's western pyre could be mistaken for the radiance of its eastern resurrection. When at last the sun does set, the sky becomes an inverted sea, whose shores are red with rocks. Two stars swim by, that might be fishes. Suddenly a hilltop house flashes the first lamplight, swift as a glow-worm. Trees lose their greenness, and loom like black lace against a grey background flushed with pink. Cool air collects in highbanked lanes where dew gathers while the bats flit. More stars appear, playing hide-and-seek among treetops whenever the breeze sighs in its sleep. They are Milton's stars,

> That nature hung in Heav'n, and fill'd their Lamps
> With everlasting oil, to give due light
> To the misled and lonely Travailer.

The sands are cool now, and the sea calm. The last yacht has lowered her sails. The lighthouse winks a rhythmic eye, carving ebony water with a white spear. The farmer prepares for bed, though his cattle still chew a moonlit cud. Unheard since early morning, the brook raises its voice from the valley, resolute as a speaker who has outspoken the hecklers. Somewhere a late thrush sings solo to a silent world, and then, receiving no answer, itself falls silent. But in the beechwood a homeward villager halts, watching the shadows that improvise inaudibly on Debussy's *Au Clair de la Lune*.

An Evening on Parnassus

I did not wish to go, yet felt that I must, chiefly because some friends had obtained an unsolicited invitation for me. So, on a sunny afternoon, I drove through the lodge gates and thence to the Hall, a Tudor mansion, whose doorway carried a large banner, inscribed with the words *Festival of Contemporary Art*. The car park was supervised by a white-faced person wearing mauve trousers and a pink shirt. After some indecision, I concluded that the person was male but not masculine.

Among the crowd were half a dozen villagers who worked on the estate, and had been co-opted willy-nilly into the *Kultur-kampf*. One of them was a gardener who used to live in my own part of the world. I found him gazing respectfully at the Sculpture Section, which contained several unidentifiable objects, some of stone, others of bone, and two that had formed part of a bicycle.

Striving to broaden my receptivity, I remembered that many composers and almost every major English poet had at some time been derided by the critics. I remembered also Wordsworth's eclectic courtesy when he said that in matters of taste the best guide is "a disposition to be pleased". Finally, I remembered that it had never been my custom to praise a poem solely because it was old, nor to dispraise a symphony solely because it was new. Thus forearmed, I entered the 'Painting Today' Section, and found that the largest canvas showed a six-legged cow with udders where her rump ought to have been. While I was unravelling the subject of the next picture, the gardener nudged my elbow. "Ullo, sir. Didn't expect to find *you* at this circus." He lowered his voice. "But don't tell 'em I said so. I work 'ere nowadays, doing the fruit and veg." He stared at the sexaped cow. "Somebody's barmy. Either them or me." Then he glanced at his sausage roll. "The grub's all right, though. Ah, and she gave me a quid to get my suit pressed. 'Don't forget,' she said. 'hart his heveryone's privilege.' "

She, I felt, had spoiled a good case by overstating it. Isaac Newton, you remember, dismissed all poetry as "a kind of ingenious nonsense" . . . an opinion which some people project on to every art. If, however, you regard art as a near-necessity, without which our enjoyment and endurance of life are impaired, then you will wish the people to have art, and to have it more abundantly than they did in the village of my boyhood, where farm labourers lived and died as strangers to art, not because they spurned those things or were congenitally incapable of enjoying them, but because many of the things were out of reach at a distant concert hall, or museum, or theatre.

My reverie was interrupted when a loudspeaker warned us not to miss the lecture on 'Poetry Today', which would begin at 6.30, after we had supped on the terrace. So in I went, to hear a shaggy youth announce that poets must henceforth discard what he called "the outmoded rhythms of a dead past". Once again I broadened my mind, this time by recalling Rimbaud's maxim:

Il faut être toujours absolument modern, "We must always be absolutely modern." Alas, the exercise failed because I soon found
myself asking what on earth Rimbaud had meant. Must we, for
instance, forego Spenser and Chekov in order to search the book
page for the names of their absolutely modern successors? Must
we banish Bach and Rubbra in order to crown Bartók's ultimate
and electronic heir? When did absolute modernity start, and (no
less important) when is it likely to end? At all costs we must
avoid being duped by a *fin-de-siècle.*

After the lecture our hostess appeared, and at once recognised
her gardener despite the pressed suit and brown boots. "Ah,
Perkins," she exclaimed. "I don't suppose you've ever seen much
sculpture. What do you think of ours?"

"Smashing, ma'am," replied Perkins, who knew on which side
his beans were buttered. "In fact, a real eye-opener." Then,
glancing at me, he added: "I was just saying to this gent, I wish
I'd brought the wife along. She's quite a hexpert on statues. As a
matter of fact, she's got one of Lloyd George, showing him from
the neck upwards." Suddenly Perkins blundered. "It looks
exactly like him."

Will Perkins ever acquire a "disposition to be pleased" by
pictures of a six-legged cow and by poems that sound like un-
punctuated prose? Unless he does learn to like those things, the
purveyors of absolutely modern culture may indeed bring art to
the people, but they will never bring the people to art. Admittedly,
the esoterics of creation can be relished only by the few; yet
Shakespeare did not address *King Lear* only to the few; he
addressed it to the entire audience, knowing that all would
receive something, and that many would receive much. To
experiment can be a mark of confidence; but to assert that poets
may no longer write sonnets ... that is a mark of diffidence,
masquerading as arrogance, because it fears the shadow of the
masters, and usually ends as a compulsion to experiment for the
sake of experiment. Perkins, the Philistine, would agree with
Ruskin, the aesthete, who said: "Whenever we care only for new

tunes and new pictures . . . Art is so far perished from us; and a child's love of toys has taken its place."

On my way home I stopped to talk with a farmer who was leaning on a stile, gazing at the moor, where a segment of heather glowed in the sunset. He pushed back his cap, murmuring: "Quite a picture, eh?" For a moment I thought that he, too, had attended the festival of plotless plays and of deformed heifers; then I understood he was merely confirming that the word 'picture' is still a synonym for a good likeness of a recognisable object. Time, of course, may revise our notions of art. Perkins's grandchildren may decide that fantasies are more significant than faces, and the sea less memorable than an artist's *mal-de-mer*. But I doubt it. The face precedes the fantasy. We would rather see Niagara Falls than a painting of them. There are moments when, if only on humane grounds, we wish that Kafka and Housman had confined their privacy to the analyst's couch. Unless the artist is a Goethe or a Wordsworth, we soon tire of his personal conflicts. Meanwhile, the cows in my own part of the world remain stubbornly quadruped; Aeschylus continues to brace them that have ears to hear; and the longest-running plays are by Shakespeare, who, although he was sometimes too lazy to invent a plot, always managed to borrow a good one. Artists soon reveal whether they are simply copying the past, or whether, like Vaughan Williams and Emily Dickinson, they are setting their own imprint on forms of pleasure which art once gave, and continues to bestow:

> So long as men can breathe, or eyes can see,
> So long lives this, and this gives life to thee.

On what day did those rhythms become outmoded? On whose authority? On what assumption?

Sitting in the Sun

In June the sun asserts itself. From being warm the earth grows
hot. Sitting in that heat, you feel the rays as though they were a
solid mass, pressing lightly and agreeably on your face. When
Chaucer awoke to a summer morning, he was enchanted by the
bright blue sky:

> The Sunne shone
> Upon my bed with bright bemes
> With many glad gilden stremes,
> And eke the welkin was so faire,
> Blew, bright, clere was the air.

Country people are less self-conscious than townsfolk in the
matter of sunshine, probably because they receive more of it.
Even when May does go out, the average farmhand seldom casts
more than one clout . . . his jacket, perhaps. Some of the veterans
merely roll-up their shirtsleeves, or remove the stud from a tieless
neck, so that their bodies present a skewbald appearance, being
the colour of mahogany from scalp to throat and from elbows to
fingertips, but elsewhere as white as nightwatchmen.

Coleridge took care that his son should grow-up in the country:
"For I," he sighed, "was reared in the great city . . . and saw
naught lovely but the sky and stars." To deep countrymen a city
in summer seems insufferable. The air lacks vigour. There is no
body to it, no honeysuckle, no hay, no seaweed. None among the
myriad streets reveals a range of mountains. No man greets
another above the din, for all are strangers. Town life in summer
negates a holiday mood. Every uncongenial task becomes more
tedious when the sun shines. People feel stifled. They dream of a
landscape whose rustic characters spend their days in rest and
quietness, immune against sickness, untroubled by age, destined
to pass peacefully from terrestrial to Elysian fields. Country life,
by contrast, has been in festive mood ever since April clothed the
hedgerows. On sunny mornings the village saddler sits outside
his shop, stitching a stirrup leather. Such postmen as still walk or

cycle, do so to the lilt of whistled tune. Housewives spend an enjoyable half-hour complaining to the woman next door that they never seem to have a moment to themselves. Pensive as Rodin's *Penseur*, old men lean on ancient gates, reciting a vista which they know by heart. Haymakers rest beside a brook, or in the shade of a tree, enjoying the sort of picnic that would cost a townsman several gallons of petrol. Ambling home through the woods, school-children play games that cost nothing except fresh air, high spirits, and an imagination that has not been stunted by expensive toys. Truly progressive teachers—in Peakland, say, or among the Cairngorms—declare an occasional *dies non*, forthwith leading their flock to browse the meadows of botany, ornithology, parish boundaries, cromlechs, mill leets, castles, coves, and many other aspects of human ecology; to which the pupils respond in an up-to-date vernacular: " 'Tis better than they daft old sums he do give us. I said to my Dad yesterday, 'Have 'ee ever needed to know what x minus y is? If 'ee have,' I said, 'then you'm a strange sort o' gamekeeper.' "

The sun does not shine on Britain with egalitarian fervour. Parts of Lancashire enjoy less than 156 hours of sunshine in June, whereas parts of Devonshire enjoy more than 236 hours. No corner of the kingdom, however, is utterly bereft of warmth. Even the north face of Snowdon acknowledges the temperature by thawing the snow. Seventeen hundred feet above sea level, Exmoor quivers in the heat. Heather is hot to touch. Winter's wet gullies are dry as dust. Ponies lie low and sometimes flat-out, dreaming so soundly that you may tiptoe within a dozen yards before the sleeper ups and aways with a startled neigh.

Sunshine enhances whatever is most pleasing, and will often uncover hidden attractions. Haworth—that grim and gritstone village—softens its demeanour in June. The moors beyond Haworth create an idyll which Emily Brontë depicted when she imagined a sun-worshipper "lying from morning till evening on a bank of heather in the middle of the moors, with the bees humming dreamily about among the blooms, and larks singing high up overhead, and the blue sky and bright sun shining steadily and cloudlessly." Her own spirit soared above passivity, delighting rather in the wind that tempers the warmth: "the west wind . . . and bright white clouds flitting rapidly overhead . . ." Being a poet, she craved the company of singers: "not only larks, but throstles, and blackbirds, and linnets, and cuckoos pouring out music on every side . . . and the whole world awake and wild with joy." Edmund Spenser so worshipped the sun that he waited on its rising,

> Early, before the world's light-giving lamp
> His golden beam upon the hills doth spread . . .

Thomas Campion did the same, adding a rebuke to lie-abeds:

> See how the morning smiles
> On her bright eastern hill,
> And with soft steps beguiles
> Them that lie slumbering still.

We use the word 'sunny' to describe those equable temperaments which generate their own inner light, and are able to flash it over a February flood and through a November fog. Come rain, come shine, they go about their business, or face the failure of it, with enviable poise and quiet good humour. Most other people are less serene. They suffer a manic-depressive cycle, feeling downcast by grey skies, and uplifted by blue ones. Some natures frown on any kind of innocent pleasure, and are never wholly at ease while sitting in the sun. Such self-indulgence, they fear, interrupts their obsessive busyness. Wisdom, on the other hand, allows that a particular retreat may form part of the general advance. We all know that Jack becomes a very dull boy when work leaves no time for play. Jack himself knows it, which is why you will find him asleep beside a hayrick, taking his ease after a morning's mowing. "To work," said St Benedict, "is to pray." After prayers, the country people turn the sunshine to another advantage, using it as a background for their play and their repose. When Wordsworth cited the "best moments of a good man's life" he did not exclude the hours that are spent sitting in the sun. On the contrary, it was from those hours that he reaped some of his finest poetry:

> ... made quiet by the power
> Of harmony, and the deep power of joy,
> We see into the heart of things ...

The Oldest Inhabitant

We emerged into the sunshine, harrowed by what we had seen in the geriatric ward, where dithering minds and decaying bodies awaited the end, sometimes begging a doctor to hasten it. Suddenly one of us said: "Let's go and see him." So we went, and found our old acquaintance sitting on a seat beside the thatched porch. The seat itself, he reminded us, was his first attempt at carpentry, completed eighty years ago, on his ninth birthday. When we asked him to tell some more tales of his life as a fisherman, he merely smiled, saying: "I'm one o' the lucky ones." He meant, of course, that in his ninetieth year he could still read a newspaper, still smoke a pipe, still walk a mile, still hear a thrush.

Three of his five children are alive; twelve of his grandchildren; and six of his great-grandchildren. Some old people outlive all their relatives, a misfortune which caused Edmund Burke to cry: "They who ought to have been to me as posterity, are in the place of ancestors." Conscious of his own good luck, the fisherman—so far from being a burden—enlivens his friends with reminiscences as racy as those of the old men in Ernest Rhys's poem:

> We have seen horses swerve,
> And vessels sail,
> We know the crimson curve
> Upon a young girl's cheek.

The fisherman lives nowadays with his eldest daughter, a widow of sixty. "I get three meals a day," he told us, "and I don't have to cook any of 'em. If I need a clean shirt, I just open the chest o' drawers. And on most mornings the two littlest great-grands come to see me. 'Tis what I do call a *real* home for old folks."

Listening to his talk, we wondered whether any other genera-tion had ever witnessed such changes as were multiplying all around him. When he first went to sea, the waves were ruled by sail. He was thirty years of age before he saw a car; thirty-five before he heard an aircraft; and nearly forty before an invisible voice said: "This is 2LO calling." His own voice roused us from our reverie. "Some of these yere railways weren't built when I were a nipper. No telephones neither. And the Queen were twenty years younger than what I am now." He added a timely postscript: "Queen Victoria, that is."

We waited, hoping that his memory was in good form that afternoon. We were not disappointed. "I began to earn my keep when I was five or thereabouts. Th'old vicar's wife her gave us a penny for scaring the birds at cherrytime." When he was ten he left school. "Ran away, in fact. But they never found me, 'cause I were serving as cabin boy in a ketch, plying between Ilfracombe and Cardiff." When he was eighty he retired. "We were lying off the Mumbles one day, and suddenly I said to myself, 'Joshua,' I said, 'you'm overdue,' I said. 'You've been at the helm long enough. 'Tis time to make way for the Watch Below.'" Instead of causing resentment, or a sense of futility, retirement has sustained his health by enabling him to fulfil certain household chores, and to take a detached interest in events; which set us thinking of Jung's psycho-philosophical verdict: "Meaninglessness inhibits fullness of life and is therefore equivalent to illness." The fisherman certainly faces facts, both past and present. "The England that I knew had a lot wrong with 'en. Poverty and disease, for one thing. And a sight too much bowing and scraping. But England doesn't exist any more. Not what I call England. Foreigners everywhere, motor cars everywhere, bombs everywhere, strikes everywhere, and our own fishing fleet harried on the high seas 'cause the English have got no guts and no guns and no gumption."

Although Bishop Ussher computed the age of the Earth, he refrained from guessing the date of Adam's funeral. Abel, we know, led a short life; and it seems likely that Cain did not lead a long one.

> That time of year thou mayst in me behold
> When yellow leaves, or none, or few, do hang . . .

Shakespeare heaved that autumnal sigh when he was about thirty years old. Two centuries later, Gilbert White gave a comparably brief life span to his own Hampshire neighbours:

"A child born and bred in this parish," he reckoned, "has an equal chance to live forty years." Yet our fisherman had lived to see an England where most people in most villages expected to reach three-score years and ten.

By the time he is fifty a man's future has become shorter than his past. Eager to discover for whom the bell tolls, elderly country-folk scan the obituary column in their local newspaper, finding, perhaps, the name of a lad with whom they shared a school bench seventy years ago, or the name of a girl they courted when she was sixteen. Few things in literature are more poignant than the surprise of Shakespeare's veteran when he learned of the passing of a lifelong friend: "What, is old Double dead?" The fishing veteran, however, remains keenly aware of his own mortality. "At my age," he told us, "a chap don't need no calendar. He times his life with a stopwatch." Even at sixty it is difficult for a hale person to imagine a routine which lives literally from day to day, and seldom with any objective other than food and sleep. Neither religion nor philosophy can wholly relieve us of an ancient dilemma. On the one hand, we fear to prolong life: "Remember thy Creator in the days of thy youth, while the evil days are come not, nor the years draw nigh when thou shalt say, I have no pleasure in them." On the other hand, we fear to lose life: "Truly the light is sweet, and a pleasant thing it is to behold the sun." Old age burnishes the distant past. Sometimes, indeed, the past has been so vividly imprinted that the image survives untarnished, as when the fisherman referred to "the new Fox and Hounds" despite the fact that the inn was rebuilt or made new seventy years ago. Nevertheless, in his own childhood the place *was* made new, and therefore it never grew old.

Second childhood, like the first, requires much sleep; and after about an hour the old rememberer began to nod. So, having said *au revoir*, we wondered how ourselves would fare in ten years time, or maybe less. But to one another we said nothing, except those spontaneous truisms which by definition are not false. We all agreed, however, that the oldest inhabitant really was one of the lucky ones, being blessed with good health, a quiet mind, and the conviction that his unremarkable life would not pass unnoticed by the President of the Immortals.

Babes in the Wood

The garden is separated from the wood by a drystone wall, one foot high, which was intended rather to mark than to assert the boundary between my own land and Farmer Zillah's, for we are such good neighbours that she allows me to trim those parts of her wood which adjoin the garden; a task not to be expected of any hill farmer who is already burdened by other and more urgent duties.

Now you would expect the birds to fly over that wall, as indeed they do, *en route* for the food and water which I provide. But they also *use* the wall, by which I mean, they either swoop down on it or hop up to it. No doubt they find insects among the miniature flower beds that stand at intervals along the top of the wall. The latest hopper—it arrived three minutes ago—is a young nut-hatch, whose nest can be seen from a window in my study. Since the species do not breed after the end of May, and since nestlings learn to fly within a month, this particular bird has already acquired so much confidence that the father appeared, warning his offspring *not* to feed beside any deckchair containing a human being. The fledgling obeyed, and forthwith returned to its tree; which led me to suppose that the generation gap is narrower among birds than among men. But not even the birds are always obedient, because the fledgling has just returned, and is once again gobbling crumbs beside my chair. During his previous absence I opened a notebook, and am now trying to write without visible movement. The father has come back, a handsome fellow, blue-grey above, pale brown below, with a black stripe round his eyes. Now they both fly away, up to their nest, where, no doubt, the fledgling will again be reminded that to crack nuts in a tree is less dangerous than to peck crumbs on a lawn.

Soon after that incident some other babes emerged from the wood; first, a young lizard, come to sun himself, then a young squirrel, which, when at last he did see me, twirled on his axis, and was away (as the Irishman said) Jacker-than-Robinson. The wood itself contains bluebells; and they, too, seem babes insofar as many of them are only a year old. Their flowering in May was a reward for my efforts during the previous summer, when I sprayed the brambles and undergrowth. Freed from the entanglement, the flowers advanced like a blue tide that became a lagoon. The wood has twice harboured unwelcome babes who wandered from their herd, invading the whole garden and the paddocks beyond. Prompted by an insurance company, the culpable farmer reinforced his barbed wire, whereafter the wood ceased to receive young stock from distant fields.

A copse is soon traversed, and forests are too vast to be personal friends; but a small wood combines concision with companionship. This wood, for instance, is scarcely three hundred yards long, and only about one hundred yards wide, yet decades of *laissez-faire* have achieved an apparent density wherein five old oaks create a Sherwood Forest, and a short tract of grass makes a miniature glade. There is, too, a sufficient variety of holly, ash, elm, thorn, bay, elder, beech. When I first came to live here, Farmer Zillah assured me that my property enjoyed the use of a private footpath through the wood, offering a short cut to the pillar box a mile away. The path, however, is very steep because it runs parallel with, and ultimately dips down to join, a 1-in-3 lane. Despite its steepness, I began to use the path, chiefly in order to maintain the right by trampling the undergrowth which concealed it. In dry weather the going is reasonably good, but in wet weather the steepest sector resembles an obstacle in a cross-country race. Experience soon convinced me that gravity sometimes defeats brevity; so, whenever the footpath became mud-bound, I took to walking down the drive, away from the pillar box, and then joining the lane on the far side of the wood.

No matter how small it is, every wood lives a life of its own, conspicuously different from the domesticated routine of gardens, or ploughland, or pasture. On Salisbury Plain, miles from any house, you can feel naked; yet in a suburban copse, flanked by villas, you feel private and alone. Squirrels and birds are the lords of woodland creation, under whom dwell innumerable insects, including those black-and-yellow beetles, called *Necrophori*, which combine the roles of grave digger and sanitary inspector, burying dead rabbits, stoats, weazels, mice. Woods are mysterious. Even a forester looks up when he hears footsteps through the leaves . . . a bird's footsteps, of course, yet so like a trespasser's that the listener thinks twice, before deciding that all's well. At midnight the mystery deepens, especially when a full moon casts silvery shafts through ebony branches.

Sometimes the wood invites a human babe, as when I am visited by a seven-year-old who enjoys the peppercorn tenancy of my vacant hen house, which now bears a painted sign, *Sarah's Cottage*, and contains a table, a teapot, a flower vase, a broom, a duster, two chairs, and *Winnie the Pooh*. There, with a doll, young Eve rehearses her domestic destiny. At seven years old a country child has not yet lost that sense of magic which adults once possessed. The other morning, for instance, my young visitor exclaimed: "I heard an enchanting sound in the wood." She raised a forefinger. "There it is again. Listen!" Her parents and I did listen. The sound, we agreed, was a prosaic fowl, just audible from a field in the valley; and, of course, the child knew that it was a fowl. Yet she said again—choosing the epithet with spontaneous deliberation—"An enchanting sound." And she was right, because the crowing did not seem in the least prosaic; nor did it observe the usual rhythm; on the contrary, it was brief, and occurred at long intervals, when we had ceased to listen for it, so that each recurrence came as a surprise. No doubt a physicist could confirm that the sound was affected by its upward drift through leaves and among branches; but the confirmation would neither lessen nor account for the effect on imaginative ears. Which is the more remarkable: a child's ignorance, or its wisdom?

7

Current Affairs

History does repeat itself, and will continue to do so until men no longer repeat their familiar patterns of behaviour. History, after all, is the record of human behaviour. During Hitler's war, for example, men returning home on leave confessed to a sensation of unreality while the train carried them through placid cornfields. Whenever they stopped at a rural station, the war-weary travellers could not help feeling that the farmfolk ought to become more directly involved in the battle. We may sympathise with their attitude despite the irrationalism. And it certainly is irrational, for even when we expanded our wartime agriculture, we still came close to being starved by German submarines, and would have been starved if the farmfolk had faltered. In that sense, therefore, Hodge was involved as deeply as the fighting men, yet the irrational attitude persists, disturbing many sorts of people.

The other morning, while newspapers were loud with wars and strikes and explosions, I whistled the dog, and walked through the fields of ripening oats. After a few miles I passed an elderly cottager who was mowing her lawn.

"Lovely day," I remarked.

The woman nodded absently, causing me to feel that I had uttered an irrelevance as well as a commonplace. Then she revealed the source of her preoccupation. "Our radio has gone wrong," she said. "Did you happen to hear the nine o'clock news?"

"Yes." I replied. "And it wasn't very cheerful."

"I don't usually get in a state about things," the woman added. "But . . . I don't know . . . I feel somehow we ought to be *doing* something. But what *can* we do? Ordinary people, I mean?" Suddenly she glanced at the sky, as though she had only then heard my opening remark. "Yes," she agreed, "it really is a lovely day. Those elms look beautiful with the sun on them. And the rain we had last night did a world of good. We were getting quite worried about the water level."

I continued my journey, reflecting how difficult it is to give the right amount of attention to the correct kind of events, and then—no less difficult—to achieve a just attitude toward them, neither sticking our head in the sand nor chopping it off lest someone else tries to do so. In achieving their own attitude, our forefathers enjoyed certain advantages, which we have cast away. Thus, crofters in Caithness knew nothing of the Battle of Hastings until about the year 1068; some never heard of it at all, and died without knowing that Duke William existed. Even during the twentieth century it was possible for Britons to go about their business unharried by the latest disaster. News of the sinking of the *Lusitania* was a week old before it reached the remotest farm on Exmoor; and even then it arrived *viva voce* through the postman, the policeman, and a shepherd who chanced to pass by. Our present rustication is very different. Every hour of every day the BBC loads us with the burden of Atlas. Some of its programmes are interrupted by an uncommercial break, during which we hear that a child died when a gangster ran amok in Los Angeles, and that Sir Timothy's pleasure-boat foundered off the Manacles: sad events indeed, yet we did not cause them, we cannot mend them, we shall not remember them, because, an hour later, they are obliterated when we hear that Perks the prizefighter has been killed by his own drunken driving, and that Pam the Protester has set fire to the Albert Memorial. Many scientists and philosophers deny that we were designed either to do or to be anything at all. Design, they say, is a plaything for artists, and purpose is the illusion of parsons. Some doctors take a contrary view, and will tell you plainly that we were designed (or have contrived to design ourselves) in such a way as to be deeply affected by anxiety. Consciously we may relish a daily diet of disaster, but unconsciously we fail to digest it, so that the unwieldy mass poisons the system, even among people who ought to be enjoying their summer garden. Yet the July sun has buried many a crisis, and its splendour is best appreciated by those who, having poured reasonable hope on the waters of justifiable anxiety, await an issue which they cannot influence.

Our only sure defence against disaster is to restrict its effect on us, by rationing the amount of attention that we give to it. Admittedly, there are some whose vocation compels them to brood on bad news. They include journalists, politicians, diplomats, financiers, the armed forces. Others are less compelled to brood. They include farmers, foresters, nurses, mothers, shopkeepers, teachers, doctors, artists. Only the very old and the utterly demented can escape some degree of anxiety concerning the world, but the world itself will in no way be helped by people who allow it to impair their efficiency by disturbing their equilibrium. While enemy gunfire shook the houses, Beethoven composed great music. Jane Austen lived through the Napoleonic Wars, yet never mentioned them in her novels. America's greatest poet, Emily Dickinson, did not write a single line about politics. Was that 'escapism?' Or was it genius and common sense, bravely abiding by their own innate priorities?

Hearing a distant church clock, I decided that I had walked far enough; so I turned back, admiring the moorland heather, yet remembering the wars, earthquakes, murders; the men who incite violence by refusing to resist it; the men who imperil the kingdom by disrupting the manufacture and sale of goods and services wherewith we buy our daily bread. If shoulders could have shrugged-off that burden, mine would have been the first to do so, because a little suffering goes a long way, whereas joy, when it does appear, seldom lingers long. The French have a mordant phrase, "The bitter taste of reality". There is, however, a difference between accepting the bitterness and declining the sweetness. A countryman finds solace in the beneficent aspects of Nature, its cyclic sleeping and waking, its scents and colours and sounds. He is strengthened by the outward and visible signs of the inward and spiritual grace with which his forefathers fought and yet defended Nature; their farmsteads, canals, hedgerows, shippons, churches, harbours, roads, parks, palaces, castles, almshouses; all the patchwork that was stitched painfully down the ages, transforming swamp and forest and wasteland into a balanced and fertile economy. No matter what he may believe about his ultimate fate, a countryman finds in Nature an unfailing source of strength: "Come unto me, all ye that labour and are heavy laden, and I will give you rest."

Still Glides the Stream

It suddenly occurred to me that Wordsworth may have rested where I was resting, on the banks of a river which flowed so fast and over such waterfalls that it sent up what Wordsworth himself called

> A cloud of mist, that smitten by the sun
> Varies its rainbow hues.

This was Lancashire, a county seldom rated as beautiful, though Jane Carlyle said that it contained England's most attractive village; and both Ruskin and Beatrix Potter went to live there, near the mountains through which the River Duddon flowed, past Seathwaite and Ulpha, into the Irish Sea. Whether Wordsworth had shared my resting place or not, he knew every yard of my journey over Wrynose Pass (where Lancashire meets Westmorland and Cumberland) and thence down to Cockley Bridge, all the while accompanied by mountains. Most people will say that Westmorland and Cumberland no longer exist, and that Lakeland has been co-opted as part of a new region, Cumbria. I say so myself, when addressing letters; but on other occasions I use the names which Westmorland and Cumberland have borne for many centuries.

Rinsed with spray, meanwhile, the waterside grass was vivid and springy. The trees shone, not yet touched by autumn, but already wearing the dark green of high summer. Birds moulted silently. Even during April it would have been difficult to hear them above the waterfall, which was compressing the river into a white spout flecked with creamy turquoise. Knowing that throughout July the river bank becomes a car park, I had arrived before breakfast, in time to see the river which Wordsworth saw. As a child, he tracked the Duddon toward its source near the foot of Wrynose Pass; as a man, he honoured it with thirty-four sonnets, a tribute unique in literature. One of the sonnets salutes his friend, Robert Walker,

> Whose good deeds formed an endless retinue.

The riverside lane led me to the hamlet of Seathwaite, where Walker served as curate of a small church (since replaced by another), in which, as the son of a peasant-farmer, he had received an elementary education from the parson. Lakelanders still call him 'Wonderful' Walker, not without good reason. On a yearly stipend of £5 he married a local maidservant, and raised eight healthy children, thereafter increasing his stipend to £20 by renting a few acres, whose produce he carried on foot, over the mountains, to Ambleside market. While Mrs Walker wove wool from the sheep, he made the family's shoes from the hide of his cattle. Besides all that, he not only became a sound classical scholar but also taught the village children to read and write, in the church where he received his own first lessons. Too poor to buy furniture for the school, he used the altar as a desk, and sat his pupils in the pews. On behalf of one of those pupils he sent a letter to the Archbishop of York: "The bearer (my son) is desirous of offering himself candidate for deacon's orders at your Grace's ensuing ordination." Every Sunday he gave hot soup to cottagers who were poorer even than himself. He acted gratis as their physician, lawyer, letter writer; helping and being helped at haytime, lambing, shearing, dipping, harvest; deserving Wordsworth's epitaph:

A Pastor such as Chaucer's verse portrays . . .

Seathwaite parish register contains this notice: "Buried, June 28th, the Rev. Robert Walker. He was curate of Seathwaite sixty-six years. He was a man singular for his temperance, industry, and integrity."

Since a Lancashire accent is nowadays regarded as the voice of broad comedy, southrons may feel surprised by Beatrix Potter's confession: "To me no tongue can be as musical as Lancashire." But the author of *Peter Rabbit* lived among the Lancashire mountains, where the accent is tinged with the more sonorous tones of Westmorland and Cumberland. In other parts of Lancashire the chief sports are cricket and football; up here they are hunting and fell racing as practised by the Tyson family, whose whitewashed farm clings to a hillside near Walker's old home. Such remote places remain strangers to the tricks of the tourist trade. Caught in a storm near Seathwaite, I recently sought shelter at a cottage. No welcome could have been warmer. "Coom een!" cried the woman. "Thee mun seet doon on't settle. Theer's nowt like a li'le fire and a coop o' summat wahming. Aye, and slip off thy jacket. 'Tis fair drooned."

From Seathwaite the river and the lane reached Ulpha, which is just in Cumberland, and almost as small as Seathwaite. Topped by a bell-turret, the white church gleamed on a knoll above the river. Inside, I noticed a pair of handcuffs that had been used when the sexton was *ex officio* the constable. Renewing old acquaintance in the vicar's riverside garden, I detected some likeness between his own pastorship and Walker's, not least in the barefoot brood of merry children. Here, also, the mountains seemed to follow me without moving. They were everywhere; etched against the sky or reflected from the river; sometimes hidden by a mist, sometimes piercing it, sometimes so clear that keen eyes could count the Herdwicks grazing near the summit.

By noon the cars had overflowed onto the river bank. Jazz whined from unmusical boxes while fag-ends and beer cans littered the greensward. Parked with their backs to the water, many of the visitors read a magazine, or dozed, or listened to the midday news. In short, the Duddon was a noisy playground. Two hours had advanced the calendar by two centuries, outdating Wordsworth:

> O Mountain Stream! the Shepherd and his cot
> Are privileged Inmates of deep solitude . . .

Fortunately, I managed to find a nook beside a waterfall which drowned the fanfare of traffic and transistors. There I heard the river's repetitive ruminations, and watched the birds preening themselves in the spray, and recalled what I could of Wordsworth's thirty-four sonnets, and especially the last, its wistful reflection that human life has only a short stay on earth, whereas rivers outlive the centuries:

> Still glides the Stream, and shall for ever glide;
> The Form remains, the Function never dies . . .

Passing the Time of Day

On a blue sky the white clouds moved like sails without a ship. Birds nearly collided in mid-air, ferrying food for a latest brood. You not only saw that the corn was thriving; you imagined you could hear it, stealthily climbing its own stalk, drawing vigour from the sun. In that sun I ambled downhill through a wood, my footsteps scattering the leaves of yesteryears. Emerging into a steep meadow, I came at last to the valley, where one farm and two cottages are arranged like particles round a nucleus of brook and bridge. Since the nearest village lies some way distant, this bridge serves as the centre of what a townsman would call 'life'. In other words, if cottagers hereabouts do assemble, it is at the bridge. You may cross it every day for six months without meeting a soul; or you may cross twice within an hour, and on each occasion encounter as many as three people passing the time of day.

The farm belongs to Farmer Zillah, some of whose sheep are folded on my own land. At this season, therefore, we meet to discuss the watering of those sheep. I had just reached the bridge when the farmer herself appeared, riding down a precipitous meadow, followed by two Dalmatians. When the pony had zig-zagged onto the lane, Farmer Zillah dismounted, and we both leaned against the bridge, eyeing the volume of water (it was ominously low), and admiring the flowers which had been planted beside the stream by Edward, a retired master of several crafts, who works part-time on farms that are lucky enough to secure his services.

"About that pump," I was saying. "It needs attention. Why not come up and have a look at it tomorrow?"

"Friday?"

"Fri . . . ," I halted. Surely tomorrow was Thursday?

"Tomorrow," Farmer Zillah stated," *is* Friday." Pause. "Isn't it?"

"Well, to be perfectly honest, I . . . "

At that moment Edward himself approached, looking younger than Father Time, and much healthier. His long-handled North Devon shovel, slung across the left shoulder, seemed the very ace of spades.

"Edward!" called the farmer. "Come and settle an argument."

Edward advanced, at his own unhurried pace, ready to deliver judgement on the prospect of rain, the age of an oak, an ailing heifer, a disputed footpath, and the best way to cure warts without wincing. Farmer Zillah then explained the nature of the problem: "Mr Peel says tomorrow is Thursday. I say it's Friday. Which of us is wrong?"

Edward drew a breath deep as Solomon's, but never a word spoke he.

"Come on, Edward. Which of us is wrong?"

"You'm both wrong."

"Both?"

"Tomorrow is Saturday."

"Well, I'll be . . . are you *sure* it's Saturday?"

"Stands to reason it's Saturday, 'cause today's Friday."

Now there are certain people—the publishers of diaries, for example, and the editors of newspapers—to whom the day of the week seems so important that only the dead or the daft can be excused for not naming it correctly. Confronted by Farmer Zillah and myself, such men will mutter: "What sort of dream world do they live in?" And, of course, the mutter may be justified. Since the week is divided into seven days, and the days into twenty-four hours, it follows that we ought to keep track of those conventions, for they facilitate the business of living. Nevertheless, we ought also to bear in mind that the sun cannot read, and is therefore unable to follow its own progress through a man-made month. Moreover, there are one or two occupations which do *not* demand frequent reference to a calendar. Professionally speaking, neither Dante nor Sibelius felt much interest in the day of the week. As for the hill farmer, only at lambing time does he suffer the nervous hurry of urban life; and even then he is not required to know the date; it will suffice if he goes the rounds at appropriate intervals. In short, there are some whose calling now and again allows them to forget that tomorrow is Saturday. But Farmer Zillah and myself are not given to prolonged amnesia. When we say "Twelve o'clock noon, next Monday," we keep the appointment, having perhaps imprinted it on our memory by recording it in our diary. For the rest, we go our own way at our own pace, living as much by the month as by the minute, and avoiding therefore Andrew Marvell's hourly obsession:

> always at my back I hear
> Time's wingèd chariot hurrying near.

A rural metabolism concurs with what Sir Thomas Browne called "Nature, that universal and publick Manuscript, which lies expans'd unto the Eyes of all." Nature, of course, is not a picture book illustrated by sentimental artists. Nature embraces disease, disaster, death. The pulse of Nature suffers many spasms, and he who lives close to Nature must share them; and the more he does share them, the more they will compel him to ask whether his own role is pointless as well as ephemeral. Townsfolk possess a keen sense of time, but little awareness of rhythm. Countryfolk, on the other hand, harmonise yesterday and tomorrow by weaving them into a cyclic present, comparable with Frank Kendon's kaleidoscope:

> And chimney smoke, and starry candle-light,
> And far-off fields, and distance like the past,
> And mossy silence, and the scent of leisure.

The man who is forever glancing at the clock becomes his own executioner. He divides life into little snippets, and then complains because they pass swiftly. Yet life flows on, regardless of the date. Monday or Tuesday, the farmer's meadow will make hay. Wednesday or Thursday, the poet's reason will make rhyme. Friday or Saturday, we shall all be dead. And on Sunday? Your guess may prove as good as mine, or better.

A Shepherd's Lucky Dip

It seems a lifetime ago since the village constable was required by law to attend the annual dipping of every flock within his jurisdiction. He usually arrived on a bicycle, his dark uniform contrasting hotly with the shirt-sleeved farmhands who drove their sheep into a chemical bath that would protect them against scab and parasites. This festival—for such it was—has from time immemorial formed part of a countryman's calendar. Thomas Tusser, the Tudor farmer-poet, advised shepherds to dip their sheep sometime in June. Nowadays the dipping takes place either in July or in early August.

With the upsurge of technology, and the elimination of scab, certain farmers decided that dipping was out of date. They preferred to use a spray. Dipping, in fact, ceased to be compulsory, and the village constable found that he could devote more time to students and strikers asserting their democratic right to destroy democracy. The new methods, however, sometimes failed to permeate the sheep's shaggy underparts. So, after all, the festival of dipping did not pass away, nor the sheep dips that still abound between Land's End and John o' Groat's. Some of those dips are relatively modern. Their concrete pavement leads to a sunken bath, wide enough to admit a sheep, yet narrow enough to prevent undue splashing. Other dips are relatively ancient, like the one beside the drove road at Cauldshiels Loch near Walter Scott's Abbotsford, which, when I last saw it, was protected by barbed wire, an iron bedstead, and lengths of timber panelling from somebody's house. Concrete paving, by the way, is not an hygienic afterthought. It is an economic necessity. If sheep are allowed to drip onto bare soil, the overflow of costly liquid is lost, but if they drip onto sloping concrete, the liquid returns to the bath. Several Exmoor farmers divert a stream into their dip, having enclosed the area with hurdles. A few weeks after dipping, the sheep are shorn; and that, too, is a rubric of the shepherd's calendar, undertaken in order to obtain the fleece and to grant the flock a cool respite from parasites. Thus relieved, a sheep soon puts on weight, and fortifies itself against the coming winter.

To all farmers their animals are a source of livelihood. To some they are mere objects, kicked and cursed by men who do not know, and could not care, that the word 'animal' comes from the Latin *anima*, meaning a soul or spirit. At shearing and dipping time even the kindliest men express themselves curtly, like the Lakeland hind who bawls at a stubborn ewe: "Thee's nobbut an owd bitch!" In Scotland a shepherd speaks from experience: "Dinna stand too close, Angus. I ken her of auld. She'd dee rather than dip." In Wales, although the Baptists are strong, the sheep still stray from the straight and narrow slipway to submersion: "There's perverse, look you. They know well enough where to go. But will they? Not unless I raise my stick and . . . get in there, damn you!" In Ireland they remember the Scriptures: "Loike a lamb to the slarther, was it? Well, all I can say is, if the Biblical lambs was anything loike me own, then the farmer must have died o' starvation afore iver he got 'em within a moile o' the abattoir." Down in Cornwall a farmer's displeasure is softened by the tones in which he utters it: "You'm that zany I've a mind to go over to beef. 'T'would serve 'ee right if I did."

The most famous of all British dippings were held during the eighteenth century, at Holkham, the Norfolk seat of Thomas Coke, who was created Lord Leicester. Sheep breeders from many parts of the world came to study his methods. A report to the Board of Agriculture stated that Coke "indulged a passion for gorgeous farm buildings." In every sense he could afford to do so. "Mr Coke," wrote Arthur Young, "readily assists not only his own tenants but other neighbouring farmers. He puts on his shepherd's smock and superintends the pens, to the improvement of his flocks, for his judgement is superior and admitted. I have seen him and the late Duke of Bedford thus accoutred work all day, and not quit the business till the darkness forced them home to dinner." All those arduous festivities were attended by the shepherd's dog, which was usually a Border collie, so eager that infirmity seldom killed the urge to serve. W. H. Hudson met a shepherd who told him that he always shot his decrepit dogs "because it was painful to see them in their decline, perpetually craving to be at their old work with the sheep, incapable of doing it any longer, yet miserable if kept from it."

Elderly people recall a time when self-employed shearers went from farm to farm, using hand shears. Here and there a farmer still maintains the old customs, but the zest has waned, partly because his car-owning men prefer to get home in time for television, partly because machines diminish the satisfaction to be had from manual skill, and partly because the ancient sense of thankfulness to God has been replaced by a profound relief whenever Chance is less destructive than it might have been. Modern pragmatism favours a private rather than a public feasting. Nevertheless, a few farmers continue to provide a shearing supper, at which an abundance of homely food and strong ale are followed by pipe-smoking and joke-cracking. In deep country, when a veteran rises to thank his master, he speaks as it were from a vanished England: "Thank 'ee for a bite o' summat t'eat. Happen the yowes will perk up now we've clipped 'em. Next thing, we'll be gathered in this barn for harvest home, and after that we mun plough with a view to scattering. And that's the way it is, the way the Bible puts it: 'One generation cometh, and another generation passeth away, but' . . . and here I'm only expressing a personal opinion . . . 'but the earth, darn it, mun be cultivated year in year out.' " That said, the shearers depart, and the veteran turns to the farmer. "Nay," he says, "I'll not trouble thee for a lift home. The night's fairing, and I like nowt better than a stroll in't moonshine. 'Tis nobbut a mile across yon dale. My own feyther walked it when he were eighty-eight, and I reckon I can walk it at seventy-six. So I'll bid thee goodnight, maister . . . aye, and missus too. That were a reet rare hot-pot she gie us."

8

The Now-or-Never Month

A party of huntsmen cantered through the heather which car-
peted the moor. Seeing them, a visitor might have supposed that
autumn had arrived, the start of September cubbing. But those
Exmoor riders were chasing their August quarry, a warrantable
stag. Even so, the summit of summer is accompanied by many
autumnal heralds. Thistles, for instance, flaunt a mauve flower;
cow parsley stands waist-high; nettles are higher still, out-
topping the wheels of a derelict wain. Blackberries bloom in three
colours—white, pink, blue—and their fruit is clearly visible,
sometimes as an unopened bud, sometimes as a berry which a
week's sunshine will redden and soften. Apples begin to blush.
Willow herb flourishes along the lane; seen from a distance, it
might be a clump of attenuated lupins. The foxglove's final
flower droops like a bell from the upper stem while the last rose
of summer waits for the sun to unfold it.

All foliage having darkened since June, it is not easy to identify
trees by the colour of their leaves. If you examine an oak, you
will notice that a leaf here and there has turned reddish-brown,
and is streaked with what appears to be a grey mould. Beech
leaves acquire a rusty border, and are pitted with holes. Already
the rowan bears berries; the 'keys' of the ash hang in clusters;

bees are busy among the lime tree's miniature fruits. Whitebrowed wheatears gather on the moor, as though to discuss their take-off for Africa. So lately a sea of grass and green corn, the land now wears a patchwork look, for the hay is bleached, and the grain is gold. According to latitude and seasonal vagaries, the tractors either turn belated hay or reap early corn. You can hear them a mile away, snorting and rattling. But whenever the breeze drops, or a driver halts for tea, you detect the stillness; not, indeed, the deep silence of September, but a murmur of insects, and somewhere a yellowhammer soliciting its familiar "Little-bit-of-bread-and-cheeeese." On cliffs above the Severn Sea a lizard suns itself; and if you try to catch it, the creature will probably escape, leaving the tip of its tail in your hand. Equally sun-loving, but far less friendly, an adder basks in the heather. Left undisturbed, it seldom bites. But beware the zig-zag markings.

Have you ever watched a great ship come alongside under her own power, proceeding so slowly that only the token bow-wave reveals that she moves at all? Such is the progress of white clouds across an August sky, stately and unswerving. Under them the horizon shimmers in the heat, so that the rim of the moor really does appear to dance a series of tiny leaps; likewise trees, houses, spires, bridges; all deceive the eye by seeming to quiver. Shadows sprawl, as if the elms had grown taller. Everything casts a shadow after noon.

August brings the sea and the moor to the peak of summer perfection. Warmed by many weeks of sun, the rocks and the beaches respond swiftly to each day's recharging of their temperature. The sea itself can become blinding when it reflects the glare. Seldom is the sky so blue, the waves so white, the surf so creamy; never so many multi-coloured sails, nor ever such a whine from noisome speedboats. Everywhere a holiday mood prevails. Asphalt promenades burn bare feet while brine stings bronzed bodies. Unvisited through nine months of the year, mountainous villages ply a brisk trade in ice-cream, sun lotion, meat pies, and picture postcards. Reapers may toil on the clifftop, and shepherds may wilt on the moor, but Britain's sunbathers lie supine in the sand, turning like a joint on a spit. The moor itself is covered with various lings or heathers, all made vivid by their four sepals of white or pink-purple. The seed is carried inside flowers which open during dry weather, allowing a breeze to propagate the species. A million seeds may be formed within one square yard of moorland. Rich in nectar, the flowers attract innumerable bees. Browsing stealthily through bracken, the deer are so well-camou-flaged that even a keen-eyed harbourer may fail to see them. Ponies, by contrast, seem less timid and more conspicuous. Unless a mare has lately dropped her foal, you can sometimes approach within a few yards of those ancient inhabitants of Exmoor. Many of them still run free, and some are rounded-up each October, to be sold at Bampton Fair.

Although the longest day lies far behind, the nights in August remain relatively short. At eight o'clock of an evening the air is still warm. At nine o'clock a hoe still clinks from a cottage garden. At ten o'clock a glimmer of sunset still steers a villager homeward from the Rose and Crown. If he has lingered there over-long, partaking too freely of its hospitality, he may be sobered—as others have assuredly been scared—by the call of a tawny owl swooping like a shadow through the trees. The white or barn owl's *kleine Nachtmusik* is not at all like Mozart's. It resembles an angry screech, brief yet piercing. Having heard it, alone in a wood, more than one reveller has vowed to sign the pledge.

Herrick's seasonal climacteric occurred in April, when he mourned the fading of his "fair daffodils". Matthew Arnold, an elegiac man, postponed his *memento mori* until June,

> When garden-walls and all the grassy floor
> With blossoms red and white of fallen May
> And chestnut-flowers are strewn . . .
> The bloom has gone, and with the bloom go I!

Edward Thomas reserved his melancholy for a later season:

Gone, gone again,
May, June, July,
And August gone,
Again gone by . . .

When July and June and May have smiled on him, a country-man feels able to accept whatever affronts are offered by August; but when May and June and July have frowned on him, he greets August as the now-or-never month, a time when summer must either appear at last or be posted as irrevocably overdue and therefore lost.

In Holiday Mood

"On holiday?" he asked.

"Yes," I answered.

"So are we. But only," he sighed, "until tomorrow. Then it's back to Birmingham." He pointed at the miles of heather and a distant sea. "Where are *you* staying?"

It would have been easy to say "Lynmouth", or "Porlock", or "Exford". But an unnecessary lie is even less desirable than an imperative one. Besides, the man and his family were friendly souls, worthy of something better than lazy deceit. I therefore explained that I lived in North Devon, and was permanently on holiday. He took my point, remarking wistfully: "Even when you're working."

Not every countryman appreciates his own good fortune. He inhabits a landscape which most other people must travel hundreds of miles to visit for a week or two each year, at some cost and trouble to themselves, and in defiance of a fickle climate. By gazing from his window, or walking to the post, a country-man enjoys those everyday experiences which a townsman rates as rare luxuries. My own encounter, for example, sprang from an interview with an odd-jobber, whose cottage bears the date 1667.

Having concluded the business, I drove on awhile, to the Somerset border, 1,600 feet above the sea, whence I sighted the mountains of Dartmoor and a glint of the Atlantic. Glancing at my wristwatch, I proceeded for another three miles, to a hamlet named Simonsbath, set among beech woods above the River Barle. Then, instead of calling it a day, I remembered that there was a full hour until noon . . . ample time, in fact, to cover the few miles into Exford, which is only a short distance from Dunkery Beacon, on whose summit you overlook both the Welsh and the Worcestershire hills. And that was where I met the man from Birmingham.

On the way home I passed two greybeards who were mowing a second crop of hay. They sweated and sometimes swore because the day was as hot as their labour was hard. Yet a holiday mood prevailed among them whenever they paused to quiz a stag on the skyline or to pat a pony peering through the fivebarred gate. Even while I watched them, the men looked up at the sun, threw down their scythes, and sprawled full-length in the shade, munching sandwiches, gulping tea, smoking shag. After a few moments they were joined by a little child who had been playing behind a haystack. To children, of course, every day is a holiday. Even at Shoreditch they use their brickscape as a playground. In this part of Britain the school bus climbs through a fairyland which the pupils need not—and, indeed, could not—imagine to be more magical than it is. At each end of their journey they alight amid scenes where summer smiles on sheep, brooks, hills. Many of the cottages are so immersed among honeysuckle that they would never be admitted into the Modern Academy of Art; and even if they produced a passport, bearing a recent photograph of themselves, still the Academy would affirm either that they did not exist or that their existence was an affront to modernity. In summer, when children and teacher have taken their fill of booklore, they go out, learning from the thing itself. Sometimes I meet them classifying seaweeds on the beach, or sketching ponies on the moor, or measuring a Celtic hill fort within sight of their village. In June the children are redder than berries; in July, as brown as nuts; in August, mahogany.

All age-groups share the holiday mood. Emerging to sweep the porch, a grandmother spends the next half-hour staking the hollyhocks, watering the roses, discussing the weather, admiring the view. Her husband cannot decide whether to mow the lawn, or to take the dog for a walk, or to watch Sam scything a paddock, or (as often happens) to stay where he is, smoking his pipe on a seat in the sun. The village shop hums with news of a world that was unvisited and unimagined by the customers' grandparents. "We'm not going to Majorca this year. My husband says he wants a change. So we'm away to Spain." "Us be taking the carryvan to Scotland next week. Sam's aunt lives near Dundee. She says there's plenty o'cinemas and such" ... "Paris is all right, midear, but between you and me I'd still rather go shopping in Barnstaple. 'Tis a sight cheaper, I tell 'ee that. What's more, they can speak English" ... "Her's taking a week in New York. Flying at the son-in-law's expense."

To all this, of course, there is another side, often forgotten by visitors who regard the countryside as Arcady, an idyll, a land flowing with milk and honey, a heaven on earth, peaceful as Nirvana, gayer than Piccadilly. The truth, alas, is otherwise, for thatched roofs cannot mend a broken marriage, nor fresh air heal a sickened mind. We in the country have our graveyards, our hospitals, our jails. We go bankrupt sometimes, and berserk sometimes, and occasionally we wonder why anyone bothers to do anything at all. The highest mountain and the deepest combe stand naked to the winds of time and chance. So-called 'rustic escapism' was a fallacy begotten of ignorance, and propagated by folly. It is the city streets, not the country lanes, which set a taboo on dung. It is in villages, not in cities, that one funeral is watched by the whole community; one scandal discussed; one feud sustained; one outcast shunned; one foundling fostered.

Although a villager could advance strong arguments to justify his preference for country life, he knows that the preference is largely a matter of temperament, and therefore partly ineradicable. He knows, too, that only in towns can a man reach the summit of his vocation as surgeon, journalist, lawyer, actor, financier, politician, civil servant. Without town life, there would have been no Dr Johnson. Hamlet himself might have rusticated at Elsinore, for lack of an East End audience. Dickens would certainly have been less prolific, and Beau Nash permanently unemployed. One might almost reverse Charles V's maxim, *"cujus regio ejus religio"*: let the faithful countryman live in the country, and the devout townsman in town, neither despising the other's preference.

The Village Fête

Soon after breakfast the sun dispersed the mist, and by mid-morning a heat haze hovered above the cottage of an elderly acquaintance of mine, who lives alone on a sequestered summit in the Oxfordshire Chilterns. I found him at his kitchen door, shaving in a small mirror propped against the rainwater butt.

"Ticklish toime o' year for water," he explained. "Especially in these chalk 'ills." The razor rasped the stubble. "Oi can git as much beer as oi warnt, but if my well runs dry oi can't git a flipping cupful o' water. Not unless oi walk to the farm. And even there the stuff isn't being chucked around." His toilet complete, the old man produced a necktie. "Birthday present from my nephew-in-law. He loikes a splash o' colour."

"Yellow and mauve," I agreed, "are very vivid."

"Thart's wart oi thought when he first give it me. But oi've got used to it now. Comes in 'andy for weddings and the British Legion."

Since his shirts were usually tieless and unstudded, I asked if he was dressing for an occasion. He nodded. "It's the village fête this arternoon. Oi'm in charge o' the coconuts." He glanced from his tie to the sky. "Charp on the radio last noight said it were going to be cool today. If this is his notion o' cool, then oi reckon a frost would bring thart old rainbutt to boiling point." Having looped his tie, he addressed the mirror. "There's toimes oi think them weather charps don't never go anywhere near the places they talk about."

"You don't?"

"Most certainly oi don't. Oi think they just ring up a pal and say, 'Wotcha, Tom . . . 'ad any rain down your way lately?' " Again he glanced at the sky. "Some o' them weather forecasts has washed-out more fêtes than the Almoighty hisself."

Suddenly a car hooted from the lane beyond the coppice. "Thart," guessed my friend, "will be the Hon."

"The who?"

"The Hon. Miss. His lordship's daughter. She always collects us for the fête. But it's a rum old crate she droives." He peered through the trees again. "Oi can see Bingo, Lucky Dip, Junior Roundabouts, and the Lemonade Tent. Thart tent she weighs near fourteen stone nowadays, so it looks loike being a toight squeeze." He darted into the kitchen, and presently reappeared, wearing a blue serge suit and a grey trilby hat, of a sort that was last manufactured about the year 1939. Stooping to flick some dust from his shoes, he exclaimed: "Oi gotta dash now, but oi 'ope you'll drop in and take a knock at them coconuts."

I followed at a distance, in time to see a greyhaired blonde standing beside a car that had been manufactured at about the same year as the trilby. The woman wore jodhpurs and an open-neck shirt. "It's a good thing I took the hood down," she was saying. "Coconuts will have to sit on Lemonade's lap." She gazed at the steep descent before them. "Don't worry about the hill. I always think it's safer to drive on the gearbox. By the way, Lucky Dip, when you hear me start up, just put the handbrake on, there's a good fellow. One can't be too careful nowadays. Right. Are we all set? Tally-ho!"

A harsh sound followed, and continued for several moments, during which the car moved forward a few feet and then backwards. When the smoke had dispersed, the Honourable was heard to remark: "There seems to be a lack of synchro with the mesh. Let's try again, shall we?" Third time proved luckiest of all, and away they went, into the sunshine and down to the village, sounding more like a rifle range than a motor car.

Proceeding on foot, I reached the village half-an-hour later, and was relieved to find that Coconuts and his colleagues were plying a brisk trade under a brilliant sky. Fate had indeed smiled for the occasion. The village green teemed with people, of whom the loudest was the Honourable herself, wielding a sledge hammer while assuring all-comers that skill, not strength, rang the bell at the top of the pole. "Dead easy, chaps," she announced. "You just give it a tap and . . . damn the blasted thing . . . jammed again. Stand back, little girl. Now! See?"

Many labours of love were making the fête a success. Someone had lent a marquee. Someone else had repaired the tea urn. A third party had supplied the crockery. A fourth was enjoying the sound of his own voice through his own loudspeaker. The millionaire's wife and her two Spanish maids were elbow-deep in washing up. The vicar had just declared the result of the under-fives egg-and-spoon race (a dead heat between both competitors). The district nurse was soliciting entries for the married women's handicap ("A married woman's 'andicap is 'er 'usband"). And two small boys were kicking each other.

The general conversation was both ancient and modern: "I wonder she had the nerve to come here. Everyone knows she's living with him" . . . "Ted swoiped a six orf the first ball, and a four arter thart, and then he himpaled hisself on the middle stump" . . . "The doctor says she's wonderful for her age" . . . "Five times I had to turn my blasted hay" . . . "I dread the winter" . . . "We put up with it till suppertoime, but when he started on Land of Open Glory, oi went up to his room, and oi said, 'Boy,' oi said, 'you can grow your curls as long as you loike, but while oi'm master in this house,' oi said, 'you will *not* play thart bloody trombone as long as you loike'" . . . "Funny, the

way we look back as we get older" . . . "Even his birth certificate
is in the wife's name" . . . "So they put their foot down and said,
'Vicar, if you burn any more o' thart incense you'll smoke out
wart few congregation you've still got.' "

It was all more egalitarian than in the years when my Chiltern
friend first went there. No cottager now feared the squire; no
schoolgirl curtsied to the curate; and everyone knew that the
Honourable had less to spend than the garage mechanic. Nevertheless, an experienced observer was able to identify the farmers,
the gamekeepers, the commuters, the colonels, the aggressive
councillor, the timid schoolmistress, the lad who would succeed,
and the man who had already failed. Despite a modern façade,
therefore, Herrick might have recognised the same kind of rustic
junketing which he saw in Devonshire:

> I sing of May-poles, Hock-carts, Wassails, Wakes,
> Of Bride-grooms, Brides, and of their Bridall-cakes . . .

Arms and the Man

The Commander was repairing his sheep dip when I came
alongside.

"Hello," he exclaimed. "I'd no idea you were in these parts.
When did you arrive?"

"On Saturday," I said.

"You've certainly chosen a warm spell." The old sailor scanned
the sky. "More like the summers of yesteryear. That reminds me,
have you ever met my grandfather?"

I paused because the Commander's grandfather had died before
either of us was born. At length I replied that I had not had the
pleasure.

"In that case, I'll introduce you."

The Commander being at all times sober, and hitherto of
uncommonly sound mind, I became even more puzzled when—

having remarked on my interest in rural chronicles—he asked whether I had seen Augustus. Again I replied negatively, adding that I had not even heard of Augustus.

"Then you'd better meet him, too," said the Commander. "We pass them on the way home. I assume you'll stay for whatever Margaret is cooking?"

"Well, it's very kind of you, but as a matter of fact . . . "

"Splendid. I hate people who dither."

My friend rinsed his forearms, unrolled his shirtsleeves, donned a jacket, and led the way to the church, which was visible in a clump of trees beyond the stream.

"Partly Norman," I observed, as we entered. "Perpendicular chancel, two Decorated windows, and . . . what a pity . . . a Victorian organ."

"It cost a fiver to instal that organ. Nowadays they'd charge fifty quid for dismantling it as scrap. God knows what grandpa would have said." My host then removed a section of drugget from the aisle. "There he is." Glancing down, I saw

> An effigy of brass
> Trodden by careless feet
> Of worshippers that pass
> Beautiful and complete . . .

Stooping lower, I could just make out "*Hic jacet*" and "*Anno D. 1387*".

"Strictly speaking," the Commander said, "he was my great-greatest-grandfather. In those years we owned the whole village. Now we've got just the farm and a couple of loss-making cottages. Still, the family had quite a run for its money. But now there's no money to run it with."

"Robert Bridges," I told him, "took a rubbing of that brass."

"Really?"

"Metaphorically, in a poem: 'It shows a warrior arm'd; across his iron breast his hands by death are charm'd to leave his sword at rest.' "

"Not bad," the Commander allowed. "He was certainly a warrior. Margaret calls him Old Turkish Delight. Damned irreverant, of course, and anyway *his* crusade was against the Syrians. He built this chapel we're standing in. And one of his descendants stuck that ghastly memorial over the pulpit."

"Sir Augustus?"

"That's the fellow. Rear-Admiral of the Blue. Ran his ship aground and then got himself appointed governor-general of a mile-long island in a half-charted backwater. Hark at him '. . . *carissimus et sapiens et benevolens* . . .' if I were St Peter I'd have told him to go back and get a valid visa. Shocking time, the eighteenth century. Almost as bad as the twentieth. I say, put that drugget back, would you. We don't want the vicar to commit hara-kiri on his way to read the Lesson."

Uninformed observers regard heraldry as a relic of feudal fey, whereas they ought to regard it as a symbol of timeless utility because armorial bearings enabled a king or a general to recognise knights who, obliterated by their visor, would otherwise have roamed round the battlefield as anonymously as a flock of sheep. Bureaucrats now classify human beings as computerised nonentities, but our forefathers blended beauty with utility. Heralds, in fact, devised a system of decorative permutations wherewith, simply by glancing at his shield, they could identify a man's lineage. The five colours which those heralds chose are gules or red, sable or black, azure or blue, purpure or purple, and vert or green. To them were added silver and gold (called "metals") as well as five furs, including vair, the material from which Cinderella's slippers were made. However, a medieval scribe mistranslated vair as *verre* or glass, whence the legend that Cinderella wore glass slippers at the ball. Not every brass is aristocratic. The church at Northleach in Gloucestershire contains an effigy of William Scors, the village tailor, with a pair of scissors between his legs. Nor are all brasses adult. The church at Collingbourne Ducis in Wiltshire contains an effigy of Edward Saintmaur, son of the Earl of Hereford, who died when he was eleven months old. Nor is every grant-of-arms a privilege of gentility. William Shakespeare, a tradesman's son, died armigerous *Non Sanz Droict*. In our own day several companies and institutions have received armorial bearings from one of two authorities: The College of Arms in England (which has jurisdiction in Wales, in Ulster, and among British subjects in Eire) and the Lyon Office in Scotland. The description or 'blazoning' of armorial bearings retains the language of medieval heraldry: "Gules on a bend engrailed argent, plain cotised or, between three lions rampant, gold, as many fleur-de-lys vert."

"Ah well," the Commander was saying. "It's time we returned to the present. I've still got six cows to milk. My Number One's on leave, you know. Spending the week at Clacton. He sent us a postcard with X marking his window. I said to Margaret, "If that was *my* window, I'd throw myself out of it.' "

9

Portrait of a Landscape

Although my dog is free from aches and pains, he has already entered his fifteenth year, and can no longer walk twenty miles a day. One mile, however, remains within reach, and this he enjoys at his own pace. Being an old man of the mountains—a Lakeland terrier, bred in Westmorland—he seems never so happy as when the wind whips his grizzled beard while he sniffs an air that is tinged with a tang of the sea. At such moments he reminds me of a lion-hearted Viking.

Despite an elegiac mood, our daily walks have their compensation because they invite me to study a landscape which hitherto I inclined to take for granted. More precisely, the dog and I follow a narrow lane to a crossroads, known locally as Muddy Patch, a good name insofar as three field-gates allow the movement of stock which in wet weather really do churn the mud. Proceeding through one of those gates, we cross a meadow, and there we sit down, as I am sitting now, in bright September sunshine, not glancing at the vista casually, but examining it, noting the details which together create an effect. The moorland skyline recalls those imperious arcs that Durer carved with his pencil, an impression of immense loftiness. The arc itself climbs gradually from right to left, culminating in a dome overlooking the Atlantic and the Severn Sea. The peaks—about 1,700 feet above those seas—are bare pasture, interspersed with heather and bog. No manmade object is visible on them. Few trees can withstand the gales there. Even the sparse thorns are mere shrubs stunted and bent. A fortnight after the last snow has thawed in the valleys, you may encounter drifts among sunless crevices on the peaks or "tops" as they are sometimes called. The moor's steepest flank is indented by a gulley, the scar of glacial erosion, whose edges are puckered, so that their shadows resemble black creases in the rock. Those heights have scarcely changed since John Leland described them in 1540: "Forest," he reported, "barren, and Morish ground, where is store and breading of young Catelle, but little or no Corne or Habitation."

Some visitors might say that the vista was impaired by high ground in the middle distance, where one of the hills attains a thousand feet, hiding part of the horizon. Natives, however, use the lesser summits as yardsticks with which to assess the giants. Basically it is sheep and cattle country, too high and windy for arable farming; the sole exception being a single wheatfield in the foreground, which shines like a golden patch on a green garment. The foothills are thickly wooded. Some of the trees stand alone in midfield, forming a shady oasis. Seen from a distance, they look as dark as late summer can paint them, but when you draw close you detect the yellows and browns of early autumn. The fertile combes and foothills are planted with hedgerows, one of which must be nearly a mile long. The fields thus enclosed run a geometric gamut. Some are quadrilateral, others are triangular, one or two are almost circular. Their pastoral appearance contrasts sharply with the high peaks, where land is divided by drystone walls. In all the vast emptiness, I see only half-a-dozen farms, all of them on lower ground. They and their sheep might be china toys. In fact, they are a Victorian legacy, bequeathed by the Knights, a family of Worcestershire industrialists, who acquired a large tract of Exmoor, chiefly in the Somerset sector. Like Coke of Holkham, the Knights transformed apparent sterility into undoubted fertility. They brought sheep and cattle and shepherds down from Scotland. They built sturdy farmsteads, walled against the wind. They metalled miles of road. They tried (and fortunately failed) to 'develop' the local mineral resources. Today, alas, other and more powerful interests are still prospecting, hoping to grow rich by scarring the scene with commercial bric-à-brac. In time, no doubt, the Philistines will declare themselves openly; and Gideon's small host will go forth to fight them.

By leaving my seat, and walking another two hundred yards, I reach a point at which the field falls away to reveal a white farm in a deep combe. That, too, might be a china toy. I can see the garden, flamboyant with flowers; a caravan; some horses; a pond with a canoe on it; and, beside the house, a 1-in-3 lane which the Devon County Council has signposted as "Very Steep Hill". Peering forward, I look down on the tops of woods and on the backs of birds flying at 500 feet. During previous walks I have sighted red deer on the heights, for Exmoor is *par excellence* their English home. Their colour so blends with the bracken that only a trained eye can spot them against September's background. They are noble creatures and controversial withal, since to hunt them is a part of Exmoor life. One stag may in one hour ruin a field of root crops, not by swallowing it whole, but by nibbling it piecemeal. Now five white clouds cross the sky sedately, as though in rhythm with Ravel's *Pavane*. There is no sound of any sort.

Returning home via Muddy Patch, with my back to Exmoor, I can see the Dartmoor mountains, nearly thirty miles away. Still there is no sound. I lean on a gate, listening; and presently I hear a breeze, and one rook, and one robin, and then again silence. It is strange to think that the windswept Exmoor skyline was popular among Bronze Age house-builders, but is now rated too bleak for a barn. I can just see some of the prehistoric sites, including a barrow and a hill fort. No road disturbs those solitudes; only such paths as were trodden by farmfolk. While roads to the coast are clogged with summer cars, you may walk all day on that skyline, probably meeting no one, possibly sighting a shepherd. The principal inhabitants are also the oldest; insects being the most humorous; sheep and larks the loudest or at any rate the least silent, for sound is soon lost among solitude. All in all, the vista combines majestic aloofness with fruitful companionship. And by way of extra it offers an awareness of the sea, a knowledge that the waves can be scanned from the summits, and that the brine can be measured on the hilltop foliage. Musing here in sunlight, I understand why Vita Sackville-West said of Exmoor: "This is the England one would like to show to foreigners—quiet, withdrawn, rather poor, but rich in tradition and love."

Tea in the Backwoods

Blackberries are a refreshing aperitif, but no substitute for buttered toast, homebaked scones, two boiled eggs, and three cups of tea. I therefore plucked the prickles from my fingers, made a napkin with handfuls of grass, and resolved never again to explore unfamiliar countryside without map and compass. Meanwhile, about a mile away, I sighted some telephone poles on the skyline. Hoping that they followed a lane, I made for them, and was not confounded. The lane itself meandered leisurely through woods, lit by sunbeams which burnished the leaves. It was all very still, very silent. Only the robins sang, sharpening their September song. After about two miles the silence was broken by the clop of an axe, so that I knew I must be approaching some kind of human habitation, if only a forester's hut. Then the lane swerved sharp left, revealing a thatched cottage in a rainbow of flowers. I knocked at the door, and was answered by an elderly woman.

"Is there," I asked, "any place hereabouts where I can get a cup of tea?"

The woman shook her head, but instead of closing the door, as I had expected, she remained there.

"In that case," I said, "perhaps you'll direct me to the main road."

Still she waited, so I explained what had happened. "I've been walking, and have managed to lose myself in the woods. How far is the nearest bus stop?"

"Seven miles," she replied. "But I will make some tea if you wish."

With a blend of reticence and dignity she stood aside, inviting me to enter. Halfway down the stoneflagged passage she halted. "In here, if you please." Ducking to avoid the rafters, I entered what I supposed would be a parlour or Sunday-best museum of lace curtains, unopenable windows, china mugs, tasselled tablecloth, and brass fender. But the room smelt fresh, alive. Its furniture was simple and fitting. A log burned in the hearth.

"What a nice room," I exclaimed, whereupon the woman nodded, or so I thought until I realised that she had made a slight bow; after which she withdrew.

Weary from walking, I relaxed in an armchair. The axe was silent now. Everything was silent. Then two embers tinkled from the logs, and some cups clinked in the kitchen, followed by the sound of a man's voice. On the Welsh dresser I noticed the faded photograph of a young girl, very gracious yet with a touch of hauteur, which led me to wonder whether the woman was a latterday Tess, descended from a line of squires. Or had she once been . . . ?

At that moment she reappeared, carrying a tray. The bread, I discovered, was homebaked. The butter and milk came from two cows in a shippon behind the cottage. The jam had been made last year. The eggs were an hour old. Only the very rich, I thought, or the rather poor, could nowadays afford to eat such fare. Having set down the tray, my hostess turned to go. When I asked her to stay she complied, but did not sit, evidently preferring to stand while we talked. Her first words confirmed my unfinished guess, for she and her husband had spent their lives in service; he as groom, she as lady's maid. Had they, I asked, been happy? After a pause, she answered: "Most people laugh."

"Laugh? Why?"

"Because they can't understand, because they never knew and don't want to know. All they seem interested in is the bad side of things, the long hours we worked, and what they call the servility." She smiled to herself. "People nowadays don't know what real work is. I'd served for three years before I took a whole week's holiday. Yet neither of us ever asked for anything in vain. To us it seemed a good life. It was natural. Everyone knew where they stood. And everyone had a chance to stand a bit higher. I can't put it any plainer than that. As for my mistress . . ."

"Is she still alive?"

"Indeed, Sir." The old woman turned to the photograph of the young girl. "What's more, she's my dearest friend. When the family were obliged to sell their estate . . . death duties, of course, and all this taxation . . . when they did sell, she went to live at a cottage in the village. Twice a week she comes here for tea, and on Sundays I cycle over to cook luncheon. This little farm . . ." she glanced through the window, "nearly five acres . . . the Colonel gave it to us just before the sale."

If you have backed the winning horse, your luck is not invalidated by the misfortune of those who picked a loser. I therefore saw no point in repeating what the woman had already stated. We both agreed that the good old days contained much that was bad; that many of their employers were uncharitable; that few pensioners enjoyed her own well-earned reward for a lifetime's service. In any event, the groom and the lady's maid belonged to a dwindling minority of countryfolk. The England they knew and loved had disappeared, the good with the bad. Nevertheless, the couple existed and were part of the contemporary scene, as real as drugged students, exiled immigrants, battered babies. Their past contentment and present thankfulness rendered them less than sensational as headlines, but even a Marxist would find difficulty in depicting them as embittered *sans-culottes*.

Swinging as usual from one extreme to another, fashion has decreed that, because many households formerly maltreated their servants, no households ought now to employ any. Human dignity, it seems, feels affronted when the doctor's wife, or an admiral's sister, says gratefully: "Well done, thou good and faithful servant." It is indeed a curious state of affairs. Public servants are regarded as laudable, even when they refuse to serve the public, and are willing to imperil its life for the price of a new television set; but private servants are regarded as despicable, especially when they scorn to bite the hand that feeds them. This state of affairs undoubtedly hastens the spread of leisure. Does it hasten also the spread of culture? Leisure is a basic condition of culture, but the hours which culture gives to floor-scrubbing are taken away from culture. Of course, when the Golden Age does dawn, everyone will spend a large part of their non-working life in the pursuit of philosophy and poetry, or so we are told, despite Freud's revelation that culture is simply the plaything of a polymorphous libido. Meanwhile, we suffer a do-it-yourself era, whose illogical conclusion will be reached when the prime minister is required by law to wash his own socks.

A Countryman's Museum

Midges circled in a shaft of sunlight streaming through the barn door. It was a Tudor barn, timbered and redbricked. The rafters had been sawn from whole trees, and their vaulting was a masterpiece of country craftsmanship. Scoured by wind and rain and frost, smothered in cobwebs and chaff, the timbers had long ago lost their lustre; but if you stuck a nail into them, it bounced back as if from a block of steel. The head cowman once told me that the wood came out of a ship which fought the Armada. When I reminded him that the barn stood more than one hundred miles from the sea, he replied by reading the inscription on one of the rafters: "ARM. DA. And there's the date, 1601." Trying not to sound pedantic, I explained that the Armada had been defeated in

1588; that DA was a variant of AD or *Anno Domini*; and that ARM was probably the initials of one of his ancestors, the Moggs, who were yeomen in the parish during the seventeenth century. The cowman received my hypothesis with the sort of lugubrious ingratitude which a child exhibits on learning the truth about Santa Claus. "In that case," he muttered, "my old Dad were plain daft. And so were *his* Dad." I tried to console Moggs by remarking

that the story need not have sprung from daftness. "Many local traditions," I assured him, "contain some truth. At the time of the Armada the squire here did serve at sea. In fact, he was wounded during the battle. He may indeed have brought home a piece of timber from his ship. But not," I glanced up at the roof, "a boatload of beams."

Meanwhile, the midges circled, the sun streamed, and a hen clucked through the chaff, winnowing with beak and claws. At

the far end of the barn, in a wattle pen, a day-old calf lay at its
mother's feet while she munched from a manger, and occasionally
peered round at me, rather as a verger might quiz the tramp who
on a rainy day has already spent three hours admiring the abbey
nave. Suddenly a mouse scurried the width of the barn, stood for
an instant on the threshold, and then darted into the sunshine.
Too late by ten seconds, a cat prowled past the open door, his
tail swaying like a submarine's periscope. When at last the cat and
the hen had retreated, and the cow knelt beside her calf, the
stillness grew profound. Somewhere a robin trilled; somewhere a
door slammed; somewhere else a telephone rang; but they all
subsided. Movement, too, subsided until, glancing through the
door, I noticed a bank of grey cloud.

"A barn," said Gilbert White, "is the countryman's museum."
This barn certainly illustrates the swiftness with which farming—
for so long a series of manual skills—became a mechanised
process. From my seat on a bale of straw I can see a new combine
alongside an old plough. On one of the rafters I see an array of
brassware that must have been the carter's pride in years when
horsepower meant Suffolk, or Cleveland, or Shire. Above the door
I see four rosettes—pink, white, yellow, blue—pinned there by
the farmer's wife, who breeds spaniels. Half-hidden behind bags
of cement, a rusty scythe lolls against a rusty sickle. Several
hurricane lamps sway whenever a breeze catches them; and they,
too, are obsolete, because the barn nowadays is lit by electricity.
Through a cob-webbed window I see nettles growing above the
iron saddle of a cultivator that was manufactured at Ipswich in
1897. If I stand tiptoe I can glimpse the hulk of a hay wain and the
rimless spokes of one of its wheels. The most interesting exhibits
are stacked in a makeshift upper storey of six planks resting on
three rafters. One of these days (or so she says) the farmer's wife
will classify those exhibits, some of which deserve a place in a
museum; the cheese vat, for example (which came from Cheshire
in 1886), and a cheese press, whose hewn freestone exerts a dead-
weight of half a ton (the stone itself stands near the farmhouse

door, and is used as a mounting block). Carefully folded, a printed circular introduces *The British and Colonial Horse Shoe and Machine Company Limited, The only Makers of Richardson's Patents and Improved Horse, Mule, and Pony Shoes . . . Contractors to many of the principal Tramway and Omnibus Companies.* In a cardboard box I find two elegant carriage lamps, and a beechwood rattle that formerly deterred birds from the cherry orchard. Today the cherries are allowed to rot because the price paid to pickers exceeds the price paid to growers. Even the cherry-pickers' ladders are rotting. A barn, however, is not solely a museum. It is a factory—a *bere ern* or Old English "barley-place"—the most important ever built by men. If every car factory disappeared tomorrow, the human race would not therefore perish; on the contrary, the number of people who died from a dearth of motor vehicles might be balanced by the number of people who did *not* die from a glut of motor vehicles. But if agriculture disappeared, mankind would soon do likewise. We can live without cars, without poetry, without music, mink coats, television, and betting shops; without food we cannot live. Bread is still a staff of life. How cynical our folly, that a jazz singer may earn more in one year than a farmhand earns during a long and laborious life.

Immersed among dusty heirlooms, I fail to notice that the grey clouds have been overtaken by black ones. Presently the last segment of blue sky is dimmed. Distant thunder rumbles, and the first raindrop plops into a tin bath beside the derelict wain. More plops follow, creating a tattoo. Chaff tumbles across the floor; the hurricane lamps creak; a loose timber thuds; straws quiver like a stirring snake. So, while the wind blows, and the rain falls, I find aromatic shelter among corn and straw and hay and roots and cake. Centuries of countryfolk found shelter in this barn, and many generations may continue to find it, for those Tudor carpenters built well, and their bricks were laid to last.

Older far than written history is man's struggle to eke an existence from the soil; older his thankfulness to see the final stook safely gathered. Barns were venerable features of civilisation when St Matthew wrote his gospel: "In the time of the harvest I will say to the reapers . . . Gather the wheat into my barn."

Dreaming of the Spring

In late September the land grows elderly, but instead of turning grey, like human beings, it goes brown. The analogy is heightened by wind-fallen orchards and stooks of corn posing as earth's grandchildren; and the birds themselves express age's love of quietude, even as the sun reflects a preference for moderation. Shakespeare's "sere and yellow" is, of course, visible and therefore undeniable, evoking autumnal sadness from summer gladness. Many people, however, achieve a second spring, not, indeed, so careless as the first fine and frivolous rapture, yet more deeply aware of profound things, and conspicuously less troubled by those trivia—a pimply nose or a torn stocking—which can transform youth's May Day into a Lenten lament.

As with mankind, so with the seasons, for September, too, achieves a second spring or renascence of activities that were assumed to be failing. If August ended as a wash-out, and September began with a gale, then Michaelmas may make amends, offering boons which summer withheld. It is offering them now, at the very moment when my wristwatch points to midday, the meridian of a sun beaming so brightly that the watch itself glints as though it were a gold ingot. Shaded corners of the garden still hold the puddles that are a legacy from spiteful weather, but elsewhere the dew is dry, the damp has disappeared, and the flowers outshine a seedman's catalogue. Dahlias are there, bruised and broken by a recent downpour. French marigolds have multiplied many times since they were planted in April, the year's first spring. Rosebuds rise above the ruin of their sires. Pansies weave a tapestry of yellow chintze, crimson velvet, white satin, sapphire damask. Dismasted and almost uprooted, antirrhinums flaunt new pennants from shattered stems. Such birds as do sing are substituting quality for quantity, led by robins that have staked a winter claim. Rooks on the opposite hill seem already to be repairing their old home; and that also is a springtime illusion. One seagull swoops like a plump snowflake, mewing the music which to seamen never sounds sad, but is a symbol of mellifluous landfalls. The gull reminds me that at the small harbour, less than an hour ago, a young yachtsman was hoisting yellow sails above a blue sea topped by the green heights of Countisbury Hill. On the jetty a berry-brown veteran glanced up from his fishing net to hail the hoister: "We could ha' done with a few days like this in June."

"And in July," the yachtsman answered. "And in August, too."

"Where are 'ee bound for?"

"Heddon's Mouth."

The old man quizzed the sky. "The glass is steady," he allowed. "But mind 'ee put-back afore teatime. 'Twill take an hour or two against wind and water."

"Not to worry. Yesterday I got back by moonlight."

"So did Columbus. But he drowned, all the same."

"Drowned? Columbus? He didn't."

"Then 'twas only 'cause he hadn't come down from London with fancy oilskins and a bookful o' theory." The sailor smiled. "But you'm all right, boy. This yere's likely to last awhile."

Presently the yacht nosed her way past the breakwater, through a line of placid waves, and thence due west towards Martinhoe and the Atlantic. Her sails billowed like a pair of primroses while the helmsman lounged at ease, open to the sun.

No part of Britain holds a monopoly of spring-in-autumn. I have found it in Lincolnshire, where the cold north meets the bleak east, on wolds which Tennyson loved. After a misty morning the sun broke through, greening the rain-rinsed meadows until they outshone April. In August a glazed sky had parched the grass, but in September the sky was a pastel pastiche of white clouds that gave the sun a wide berth. I found the same mildness in Scotland, where the Mull of Galloway creates a northern Land's End, far south of the English border. Children were paddling in Drummore's deserted harbour while the lighthouse gleamed whiter than a midnight ghost. On the Marlborough Downs I have found it, warming Richard Jefferies' countryside, coaxing rabbits to sunbathe, and bees to bumble. Beside the Thames I have found it, along that sylvan reach between Medmenham and Fawley, where the Chilterns come down like cattle to drink, their leaves almost lapping the water. For an hour I sat there, steeped in sunlight while the glittering river answered Spenser's prayer:

> Sweet Thames! run softly till I end my song.

Do you know Dale, the sunniest spot in all Wales? There, too, I have found a second spring, this time beside salt water, whose waves were creamy ripples flecked with gold. I found it once in Sussex, along that skyhigh road from Woods Corner to Battle, where the Normans achieved a victory which we attribute to Hastings . . . Kipling's country and therefore Puck's and therefore older than the William who conquered it. In a paddock near Netherfield some foxgloves were still flowering.

Wherever I travelled, the talk was of the weather. In Westmorland a farmer spoke: "Happen we mun take a third haytime." In Wales a postman spoke: "Evan Morgan, bach, went to sell a cow, but he ended up buying a swimsuit and diving off the pier I shouldn't wonder." In Scotland a dominie spoke: "I dinna ken who'd waste saxpence on a fire this weather. It's no' as if the wood chopped itself and then paid the bill." In Kent a Cockney spoke: "We came darn 'ere ter pick the 'ops. But all the pickings I ever got was a coupla wasp bites and a pint o' sun lotion."

When summer dies, the requiem is often restful; now and again it is more restful than summer. August may chant a shrill *Dies Irae*, but Michaelmas intones a calm thanksgiving. Second spring? Indian summer? Names do not matter. In September the earth dreams of April, and (as Quiller-Couch observed) Nature herself retires in order to advance:

> She feels God's finger at the root,
> Turns in her sleep, and murmurs of the Spring.

10

On the Deep Blue Sea

A brown spot appeared on the blue sea. Since the boat was dawdling at three knots I had ample time to lean over the side, and examine the jetsam, which proved to be the leaf of a horse chestnut, sodden yet vivid after its mile-long voyage from the shore. How it contrived to sail so far was a mystery. Perhaps the previous night's gale had wrenched it from a tree and then launched it downriver on an ebb tide. Perhaps the gale had hurled it against the hull of a fishing boat, whence it slithered into the water. Anyway, there it floated, like a leaf from an amphibious calendar. Then the boat's wake raised it, rinsed it, and sank it.

The sea ahead was empty. The beaches astern were empty, too; yet six weeks ago they had been strewn with sunbathers, and two weeks ago the last sand-castler watched the hardiest swimmer. But now the Cornish Riviera stood deserted, except for some heifers which wandered from the lane and onto the beach, scrounging whatever tit-bits had been scattered by the visitors. Port and starboard the coast climbed gently, and in places created an impressive cliffscape plied by two tractors, one of which was raising a cloud of dust while the other attracted a gobble of gulls. Further inland, a hedger stroked his bonfire. Polynesian sailors might have been able to smell the distant blaze, but I could only see it, and envy the prowess of so-called 'backward people' who employ smoke as a post-free epistle. The recent gale had been local and soon spent, leaving the sea so calm that *Noah's Ark* swept it aside, lordly as a plough carving white furrows on a blue field. Three miles to seaward a tanker's portlights caught the sun, blazing as though the vessel were on fire. No other shipping appeared until a Customs launch put-out to board the tanker, which then altered course, ready for the last lap into Falmouth.

If—apart from occupational hazards—the sea does suffer disadvantage vis-à-vis the land, then it must be in its lack of a landscape. Yet I have lived the four seasons on salt water, and never wearied of gazing at it. No landscape changes so dramatically as the sea, none so swiftly. It is true, of course, that mountains wear white in winter, and that trees, having stood naked through half a year, change the colour of their leaves before the next nudity. Yet mountains retain their shape, and trees do not wander. But the sea does change shape, and is never still. On it an ocean-going vessel may crash into the troughs, or spread her wake like a Milky Way on a glassy sky.

At noon I brought the boat round, swinging through a wide arc which showed no land at all, but only a deep blue sea. During those few moments the sunken leaf seemed to have been torn from the wrong month, for surely this was not October, a specific number of autumnal days; it was summer and eternal. Then the bow sheered away from that illusion, balancing briefly on the hills above Helford River. Off Saint Mawes I encountered a mosaic of drifting leaves. Some were blackened beyond recognition; others had become so waterlogged that only their tips showed above the surface; a few identified themselves at once, like the sycamore leaves clinging to their twig. As the bay gave way to the river, the leaves multiplied; and when Percuil hove in sight, sheltered by wooded hills, whole colonies of leaves floated past, clustering like sheep for comfort. Sometimes a leaf could cluster no longer, and parted from the flock, steering its own course to its own end. In the fairway between winter-moored craft I saw leaves on tarpaulins and on combings; leaves every-where, in scuppers and dinghies and cockpits. The mast of a ketch carried two on her bowsprit, impaled like slithers of meat on a skewer. In my own boat they resembled stowaways, crouch-ing under coiled ropes, lurking on locker seats, flattened against fenders, wedged among planks, plastered on portholes, wrapped inside the pennant.

Proceeding to a berth that always holds more water than the boat draws, I went below to tap the glass. It had dropped a couple of points since dawn, and was backing to 'Change'. Still, the afternoon remained sunny, so I shook off my seaboots, lit the stove, and presently sipped sweet tea while salt water flowed beside autumn tints. Loveliest of all were the beeches, burnished bronze on polished boles. Oaks were crinkled into parchment. Cherries vied with a robin's breast. All asked an ancient question: is not October more beautiful than April?

Soon after three o'clock the sun became merely ornamental, though still bright enough to blaze a trail through the waterside woods, as if to emphasise that October brings the trees to the peak of flamboyance. November will comb them until their glory has departed, and the last leaves fall like the hairs from a man's head. One more gale, or the first sharp frost, will reveal the shape of winter, and its sound also, as Emily Lawless knew:

> Now the seagull spreads his wing,
> And the puffin seeks the shore,
> Home flies every living thing,
> Yo, ho! the breakers roar!
> Only the Cormorant, dark and sly,
> Watches the waves with a sea-green eye.

But while the pageant does last, it dazzles and delights, having this in common with spring, that it arrives punctually at a predictable season; that it has been watched many times before;

and that the sameness never cloys. Autumn's chief surprise is its ability to amaze us.

The Speaker for Tonight

The rain was so heavy that the headlamps revealed only a white wall within a few feet of the radiator. Worse still, I had trusted memory instead of consulting maps; and now the mountains mocked me with a maze of lanes whose signposts were unreadable through the downpour. In the end, I manœuvred the car until its lights illuminated the place-names, thereby enabling me to reach my destination. On arrival, however, I wondered whether anyone would be there to receive me, for I had never encountered such torrential rain, and had seldom entered such a remote village. But I under-estimated the warmth with which a rural community greets its Speaker for Tonight, even when the heavens have opened, the lanes are awash, and most people sit at home by the fire. My hosts, as it happened, were the heirs of those Lake-landers whom Wordsworth described as "shepherds and agriculturalists, proprietors, for the most part, of the lands which they occupied and cultivated." One such agriculturist had been posted as look-out in the porch of the village hall. Seeing the car, he dashes forward, brandishing an umbrella. "Eh, but thou's chosen a reet wrong 'un," he exclaims. "Dids't notice the beck, coming over Cragside? I've never knawed it flood so fast. But come on een. Theer's a full house to hear thee. Even owd parson's turned up, lumbago an' all." So saying, he conducts me into the village hall, which hums with chatter until, seeing their speaker, the audience fall silent, quizzing him with critical yet courteous curiosity.

Most of the company are women, many of them no longer young, but they have been rejuvenated by a child or two, and three hand-holding adolescents, and five young farmers with bonnie wives. In the mountains, of course, first things come first. "Dost fancy a wash?" asks my guide. "Nay? Then thou'll be wanting a coop o' tay". The umbrellaman turns to the tea lady. "Missus! 'Ees't on't boil yet?" The lady advances, whitehaired, apple-cheeked, dressed daintily in whatever fashion has climbed from Kendal or Broughton.

"Sugar?" she asks. "These lumps nowadays are that small you need a magnifying glass to see 'em. Twa? I'll gie thee fower, an then maybe thou'lt taste summat. And try one o' yon pasties. Straight from oven. 'Twill do thee a power o' good after the rain."

Thus refreshed, I hand my coloured slides to the projectionist, and then mount the platform to meet the chairman, who presently rises to introduce me. Some chairmen so love the sound of their own voice that their speech is a perpetual preamble; others are so timid that even their introit sounds elegaic. This chairman is neither timid nor prolix. His first words hit the mark. "Theer's no call to say much about our speaker for tonight. No doubt you've read his bukes, or seen him on't box. I'm sure we'd all wish to thank him for coming such a long way on such a wild night." A ripple of applause follows. "In case anyone didn't see the noticeboard, the speaker next month will be another famous personality, Reverend Bassenthwaite, him as lives agin Ulpha, and was a missionary in foreign parts. His subject will be the Gospel in Zanzibar." At that moment someone tugs the chairman's sleeve. After a whispered duologue, he makes another announcement. "I've just been reminded that, owing to the international situation and the state of the road from Ambleside, tomorrow's darts match has been postponed, but not . . . I repeat, *not* . . . the Bellringers' Beanfeast, which will take place as advertised, seven o'clock sharp in't church 'all. And now, ladies and gentlemen, it is with great pleasure that I call on our speaker for tonight."

After a few words from that speaker, the lights are lowered, and the audience gaze at the screen, eager to see the pictures which they themselves have asked to see, showing their native Lakeland. And when the last slide has appeared, and the lights are switched-on again, what a hot collation of sausage rolls, home-made cakes, sweet tea, and—the parson having departed—something from someone's hip pocket. If there are any regrets, it is only because the speaker must return to Kirkby Lonsdale, and therefore cannot accept the invitations to "bide wi' oos agin't morning."

Winter, they say, has its compensations. For me they include the pleasure of renewing old acquaintance, and making new ones, at village halls and urban banquets. Robin Hood, you remember, relieved the poor of some of their poverty by relieving the rich of some of their riches. Just so, albeit in strictly lawful fashion, I allow one lecture to subsidise several. The result may not always be what the economists call viable, but it never fails to seem variable, and by means of it I have acquired some knowledge of the state of the nation. But do not suppose that public speaking is at all times a source of vainglory, for there are times when it invites—and may ultimately enforce—a painful reappraisal of one's place in the cosmos. If any man suffers a swollen head, let him become the Speaker for Tonight in a remote place, where few people had ever heard of him until they chanced to read his name outside the village hall. He will soon discover that in those parts a man is rated rather for what he is than for what he earns, or owns, or has achieved. In Wales they put the matter very plainly: "He may be a Duke, for all I care. The point is, bach, he drinks like a fish, he swears like a trooper, and he calls himself Captain, though I know for a fact the highest he ever got was corporal in the Home Guard."

Shillings have gone, miles have gone; acres and inches and pints have gone. Our names and our customs are decimated, decimalised. England, it seems, is on the wane, outdated and soon to become archaic. But is it? I wonder. I do indeed wonder. And my scepticism is based on experience of places and people who, although they never attract the limelight, are as real and as

relevant as this morning's headlines. In them the old loyalties live
and will be handed down. The old customs live, the old legends,
the old words; not as obsolete relics of the past, but as lively
aspects of the present. Rural Britons, therefore, continue to resist
alien fashions and urban attitudes. Their obstinacy may be
mistaken; in time, no doubt, it will be overtaken; but the day has
not yet come when Cornish harbours and Kentish oasthouses no
longer care to see themselves on the village screen; when a
Welsh Women's Institute can no longer compete with television;
when the men of Donegal no longer sing of Meenaneary; when
a Scottish crofter no longer waits outside his village hall, scanning
the snow for the Speaker for Tonight.

End of an Era

The breeze seemed welcome after the languor of high summer.
It swept away the flies, rippled the sky with clouds, and set the
muscles tingling, ready for a walk through fields red with berries
and the blazoning of autumn. If, however, you still cling to
summer, you may find wisps of it, especially after midday, when
sunlight warms the last field of standing corn. August was sheer
summer; November will be undoubted autumn; but October
offers a taste of both. Awaking at seven o'clock, you are greeted
by Thomas Hood's reveille:

> I saw old Autumn in the misty morn
> Stand shadowless like Silence, listening
> To silence, for no lonely bird would sing
> Into his hollow ear from woods forlorn . . .

At ten o'clock the mist begins to move. At eleven o'clock the sun
scatters it. At noon you sip coffee in the garden. Seven hours
later you draw the curtains, light a fire, and brace yourself against
six months of snow, rain, gales, fog, mist, mud; any of which

may be mellowed by halcyon days so unexpected that you cannot decide whether they are summer's oldest inhabitant, or spring's youngest arrival.

It was on such a day that I travelled through Rutland, formerly the smallest of English counties, which, despite gallant resistance had at last been sacrificed on the altar of 'efficiency'. So—almost unnoticed by the rest of the kingdom—nearly a thousand years of pride and identity were buried without ceremony. Oakham is no longer a capital; it is simply one of Leicestershire's smaller towns. The rise and fall of Rutland deserves something better than a footnote in a gazetteer. During Saxon times the region was a soke or community of semi-autonomous freeman, not unlike the estatesmen in Wordsworth's Westmorland. The name 'Rutland' is a corruption of 'Rota's land'. Concerning Rota we know only that he was a local chieftain. Edward the Confessor granted the territory to his wife, Edith (one of the villages is named Edith Weston), and for a long while thereafter it remained an appanage of the Queens of England. In 1086 the Domesday commissioners described it as lying partly in Leicestershire and partly in Lincolnshire. King John created it a county. Six centuries later a survey for the Board of Agriculture angered the Rutland folk by remarking: "This least of English Counties is intimately joined with Leicestershire, and may be considered a natural part of it." However, the author of the survey was impressed by the Rutland landscape, praising it in language not commonly found among official reports: "a billowy sea of grazing and breeding grounds." But the Industrial Revolution was already luring farmhands "from their native and appropriate habits, to manufactures and other comparatively useless arts . . ." England, in short, had begun to put most of her eggs into one basket, trusting that by selling them she would earn enough money to buy eggs. In 1808 a second survey once again congratulated the Rutland landowners: "The management of grazing lands," it declared, "is much better understood in this county than in many others." Defoe reported that Rutland was "famous for abundance of homes of the gentlemen..." Chief among those gentlemen were, and are, the Manners family, Dukes of Rutland, whose seat, Belvoir Castle, lies just outside the county. The first Belvoir Castle was built by Robert de Todeni, Standard-Bearer to William the Conqueror. Having fallen into decay, the castle passed to the Manners during the sixteenth century. The present building was designed by

James Wyatt, a Regency architect, who specialised in medieval reproductions. The Belvoir Hunt (they pronounce it 'Beaver') was founded in 1730, as the Duke of Rutland's Hounds.

At Oakham, formerly an assize town, I admired especially the twelfth-century manor house that was fortified by the Ferrers family. On its walls I saw a unique collection of horse shoes, for the medieval citizens acquired the right to levy a toll of one shoe from every passing peer, unless he preferred to pay cash. They say that the custom was started by Wakelin de Ferrers, Master of the Horse to William the Conqueror. From Oakham I drove at twenty-miles-an-hour through trim lanes, past handsome houses, into a realm where good husbandry was still the principal occupation. A comparably well-bred neatness can be found in parts of Sussex and Kent, but there one is conscious of London commuters and of roads to the coast. Rutland, by contrast, is a deep countryside, covering less than 152 miles, and containing less than 25,000 people (one hundred English towns have each a population three times larger than Rutland's). The majority of Rutlanders look to Leicester or to Northampton as their metropolis. They possess nothing which Birmingham would rate as a factory. They are, in Cobbett's phrase, "lads of the land", countryfolk born and bred.

Rutland's most attractive town is Uppingham, where many houses are built of the local Ketton stone, flecked with pink and brown. Uppingham has been saved and also succoured by its school, which was founded by Archdeacon Johnson in 1587, and for the next three centuries prospered quietly as a grammar school. During the 1840s the headmaster, Henry Holden, applied for the vacant headship of Durham School; the only other candidate being Edward Thring, an Old Etonian. Holden was chosen, and Thring succeeded him at Uppingham, where he found one master, one usher, and twenty-five pupils. Like Arnold at Rugby, Thring made his school famous throughout the land. Whenever I visit Uppingham I am reminded of what Oxford must have been like at the beginning of the nineteenth century; rustic yet academic; a pageant of stone, built to outlive the fashion. During term-time at Uppingham you will hear young voices declining *mensa*, declaiming Sophocles, and calling loudly on Isoceles. You will see corn and pigs being carted through narrow streets. Horsemen, too, are not unknown, especially when autumn opens the hunting season. Of industry and commerce you will find no trace at all, unless you stand beside the traffic lights, seeking them. This pleasant country town was once called *Yppingeham*, the home of the people who lived on an *upp* or hill. That hill now overlooks fertile farmland, gracious manor houses, neat cottages, ancient churches, and a multiplicity of coverts that were planted for the benefit of the Duke of Rutland's Hounds.

A Gathering of the Clans

Glancing at the company, in which the ladies outnumbered the men, I noticed that I was the only male who had his trousers on. The scene, however, was not a new and indecent exposure by one of our undramatic dramatists; it was a gathering in the Scottish Highlands, at the home of a laird who lives modestly on two hundred acres, and counts himself lucky to have rescued that small patrimony from the most ghoulish of all forms of destruction, the tax on death. Among Englishfolk he would be regarded as a squireen, the descendant of a family which once owned many acres, but now possess few.

In the Highlands, of course, every laird belongs to a clan, as do most of his friends; and on special occasions, whether solemn or festive, the company wears the appropriate dress, which, for men, includes a kilt, a plaid, a bonnet, a doublet, a goat-skin sporran, buckled shoes, scarlet garters, and (on very high occasions) claymore, sword-belt, pistols. Those accoutrements were not devised as ornaments, but rather as necessities, a collective *sine qua non* for men who fought hard and lived hard, surrounded by hostile clans and snow-capped mountains. Being the only Englishman present at the gathering, I wore no kilt, because I belonged to no clan. However, the lack of a kilt did not disbar me from admiring the rainbow of tartans. 1 liked especially the colours of the MacLeod of Lewis and Raasay, whose yellow field or base was enhanced by a third red stripe. Less vivid, though scarcely less pleasing, was the Macpherson tartan with its white field crossed by wide grey stripes and by narrow stripes of yellow and cerise, or so it seemed to my own eyes; but the whole business of Highland Scottishry is so technical that an Englishman may find himself rebuked on a point of Gaelic or on a question of optics. One thing at least is certain: the Highland clans are social groups descended from a common ancestor. William Aytoun stated the fact stirringly, in his description of a Highland chief:

> He kept his castle in the north,
> Hard by the thundering Spey;
> And a thousand vassals dwelt around,
> All of his kindred they.

The Jacobite Risings caused our Germanic King to assail the clan system and to proscribe the Highland dress. Happily and predictably, his campaign failed, and in 1782 the Scots were once again free to wear their native costume. When George IV wore it, suitably corseted, he founded the tartan trade, whereafter the Great North Road bristled with commercial travellers and their pattern books. Despite her grammar, Queen Victoria was justified when she claimed that, "as representative of the Family of Bonnie Prince Charlie, no one could be a greater Jacobite than herself." As all the world knows, Victoria and Albert created their own private museum at Balmoral. But Stewartry spread far beyond Scotland. Even the Whigs became Jacobites; even the Free Trade Liberals. I have by me an advertisement which in 1903 was circulated among the merchants of Manchester. "Why not," it suggests, "have your favourite Scottish Tartan made up for use as Gents' travel rug or Ladies' bespoke skirting?" Such commercialism insults the intelligence. It is as though a goalkeeper appeared on duty wearing the Order of Merit, thereby flaunting the outward and visible sign of an inward and spiritual grace which he did not possess.

The clan has no equivalent elsewhere in Britain. Both the Welsh and the English long ago foreswore their tribal chiefs, who in any event were seldom so accessible and never so loyally served as were the Highland chiefs. The most civilised parts of Scotland are the least industrialised, and for that reason they still deserve Boswell's compliment: "Civility seems part of the national character of the Highlanders. Every chieftain is a monarch, and politeness, the natural product of royal government, is diffused from the laird through the whole clan." In current jargon, the clans' mystique is unofficial. No law allows a chief to conscript his followers for private war, nor tax them for private profit. The Chisholm remains *primus inter pares* among the many sorts of people who constitute his clan. Nevertheless, a true Highlander feels towards his chief an affection which few Frenchmen have ever extended to their President. Gunns, Armstrongs, O'Shannaigs, MacNivens . . . from all parts of the world they write to their chief, and sometimes they visit him (or her). It is as though the entire tribe of far-flung Robinsons felt affinity with one another, and owed allegiance to their chief, The Robinson of Hammersmith Broadway.

Trousered meanwhile in Sassenach isolation, I became very conscious of Scotland, not least when I wandered onto the terrace, hearing only the breeze and a distant burn. This, I felt, was a land which had retained its own laws, its own language, its own kirks, crafts, and customs. An Englishman has no answer to the kilt, unless it be to stand aloof, humming *Greensleeves*. Not even a warship's bugler at sunset sounds quite so moving as the pipers when they play their variations on a thousand years of courage and renown. Boswell was indeed justified when he said that many Highlanders—rich and poor, Calvinist and Catholic—speak and act gently. There is about them a *noblesse* which can hardly be defined. Their way of life contributes to it, even as their landscape moulds the way of life. Religion also plays a part, in some a leading part. Their recreations reflect their ethos, as anyone will discover if, late at night, he hears their regional radio; for whereas the rest of the kingdom too often suffers jazz, or politics, or Stock Exchange gossip, the Highlanders receive Evensong, or a reading of Gaelic poetry, or a recital of Gaelic music.

Threatened by a gush of North Sea Oil, the Highlanders face a threat more insidious than poverty. An Englishman, therefore, can only hope that they will retain some of their heritage as *Tir nan Og*, a land whose best aspirations do not die, but are born again with every bairn in every croft and castle and manse.

Poetic Licence

My friend the Chiltern hermit was in fine form when I called at his hilltop cottage, a remote and sylvan retreat, perched like an eyrie above the plain of stubbled wheat. I found the old bachelor hanging his pants on a clothes line. Hearing my footsteps down the grass path, he turned—still with a peg in his mouth—and nodded a welcome. Then, having secured the garment, he greeted me with his customary blend of kindness and curtness: "Keeping well?"

"Fortunately," I replied.

"If a charp's got 'is 'ealth, there ain't much else he can't do without." He peered over his steel-rimmed spectacles. "If you see wart oi mean."

"I do see."

"Been walking?"

"Yes. Along the Icknield Way."

"In thart case, oi'd best put the kettle on. Reckon you could do with a cup o' tea." He glanced down the path. "Your little dog still aloive?"

"Very much so. But he's nearly fifteen nowadays, so I left him in the car while I went walking. He still enjoys a stroll, though."

At that moment the stroller himself appeared, having been detained by a squirrel in the woods. My host then placed a saucer of water beside the garden seat. "Fifteen, eh? Thart's tickling along." The dog drank loudly. "Loike wart oi said, if you've got your 'ealth . . . anyway, we moight as well drink ours in the sun. Oi wish we'd 'ad a few days loike this in June. It's a real picture."

"A picture," I agreed, "and also a poem."

"Oi were a bit of a dab at poitry. In farct, oi once gave a public resucitation."

"You did?"

"At the school concert. And in return the vicar gave me a proize. Oi've still got it somewhere." He dragged two rickety seats into the sun. "Take a pew. Shan't be a jiffy."

I sat down, rested and restful. The encircling beechwoods shone like a veerless flame. Over the plain a skyful of larks unleashed their carillons. Wasps grew tipsy on windfallen plums while squirrels pattered through beech mast, making the most of the warmth before they retired into half-hibernation. Presently the old man reappeared, carrying two cups of tea and a small parcel, neatly tied with string. "Cheers," he said, and sipped. That done, he set his cup on the grass. "Loike to see my proize?"

"I would indeed."

"My old mother wrapped it up," he explained. First came a layer of brown paper, then a rustle of tissue. "Fair fond o' thart proize she were. 'Look arter it,' she used to say, 'because the vicar swears you're thart lazy you won't never git another.' " From the wrapping he produced a *Golden Treasury*. "Fella called Palgrave wrote this," he remarked, stubbing the flyleaf with an earthy thumb. "There's the date. Way bark a bit, eh? And there's my name. The *aetat* is Latin. It means oi were seven-and-three-quarters."

"Very creditable," I said. "What was the winning poem?"

"Oi fergit the name. But oi remember the first words. 'In Zanydu a stately dome . . .' The vicar told me all about thart poim. It was written by Samuel Coleridge, the famous tailor. And one day this 'ere Coleridge dreamed a poim about a charp by the name o' Cobbler Khan who fell in love with a maid as played a Habyssinian dulcimer. Ah, and there were another person in thart poim. A person from Porlock. Fella called Alf. He swam down a sacred river, roight as far as the sea. But oi expect you knew all thart."

"Some of it."

"Oi believe *you've* written a poitry book."

"Four, actually."

"Poitry's loike snuff. It takes a bit o' gitting used to, and even then not everyone enjoys it. My granfer didn't."

"Oh?"

"Gran went with him to London once, to see a poitry play called Hamlet. And halfway through, old granfer fair caused a rumpus. According to gran, he stood up in his seat, and pointed at Hamlet, and shouted, 'Boy, for Gawd's sake stop talking and *do* summat.' " The hermit glanced at me. "Oi see you're smoiling."

"I was wondering what your grandfather would have said to some of our modern Shakespeares. In their plays its all talk. No one is allowed to do anything."

"And yet, you know, t'warn't always loike thart. My other granfer used to go regular to the Working Men's Literary Institute . . . it's a Bingo Hall now . . . to hear poims by Lord Tennyson and Mildred."

"Mildred?"

"She were the vicar's cousin. Wrote a noice poim about a frog, oi remember." He began to re-wrap the parcel. "So you've been walking th'Icknield Way? Then oi'll tell you another thing. A long toime ago there were pedlars walked th'Icknield, carrying a pack o' pins and ribbons and suchloike. And some on 'em carried poims, too. And the cottage folk they'd buy one and share it aloud as you moight say. Oi know thart's true 'cause my father's mother-in-law found a bundle o' them poims when she helped to clear up arter the Black Bull was burned down. Ah, and she showed 'em to a charp from Hoxford, and the upshot was, a museum paid her ten pun for the lot."

He set his prize beside him on the seat, saying: "It must be thirty year since oi last looked at them poims."

"You're not the only one," I remarked.

"Oi don't reckon they'd sell much poitry nowadays on th' Icknield Way. In farct, oi don't reckon they'd sell much poitry anywhere. Not even in Hoxford. Why *is* thart?"

"Partly because of the poets," I replied, "and partly because of the public."

II

Keeping the Home Fires Burning

In the year 1526 a conference or diet was held at the Bavarian town of Spires, which reaffirmed imperial allegiance to the Roman Church. Led by the Elector of Saxony, several Princes and fourteen cities protested against that affirmation, and were therefore called Protestants, a name revered by those who annually celebrate the downfall of the most famous of all our anti-Protestants, Guido Faukes, commonly called Guy Fawkes.

If a traveller in these hills the other night had glanced toward this particular summit, he would have rated it a bastion of Protestantism because, although it held only one house, it burned three first. However, the outbreak of Anglicanism was in every sense unorthodox, having begun in mid-afternoon, to suit the convenience of certain very young Protestants from remote farms and cottages, none of whom had yet attained that state of grace which sees crackers and squibs as theological rubrics. Moreover, the fireworks themselves were neither loud nor lethal, but consisted of sparklers, catherine wheels, and one rocket whose price ensured that it would never reach the moon.

Later that evening, when the guests had departed, I went the rounds, knowing that bonfires have a habit of not dying down. The air was crisp yet cordial. Stars shone, seeming to trickle like quicksilver through the branches. Frost was at work, icing the lawn, prickling the path, crusting the pond. From its covert half-way down the hill a fox barked defiance at blood sportsmen. From the wood beside the garden an owl hooted so loudly that the sound startled me. Then the *Nachtmusik* subsided, and the hills resumed their customary silence, which was heightened by the faint babbling of a stream in the combe.

It so happened that the hedges enclosing the paddocks had lately been trimmed, and several superfluous trees felled, whereof the relics lay like a tidemark along the perimeter. For nearly a month I had shirked the task of collecting and burning the debris, but now I chucked a few twigs onto the embers, and was soon rewarded with a flame. More twigs followed, and after them a small log, and after the small log a large one, topped by a barrow-load of leaves. Just such a beginning, I thought, had prompted St James to exclaim: "Behold, how great a matter a little fire kindleth." One by one the boughs spluttered, smoked, crackled. Not Latimer himself could have wished for a brighter salutation to "the Church of England as by law established." Indeed, the fire on the ground caused a rumpus in the air when roosting birds fluttered above the wood, refusing to sing their dawn chorus for such a blatantly spurious sunrise. The cheerful glow recalled Hardy's cheerless comment on the bonfires that once warmed Egdon Heath: "to light a fire is the instinctive and resistent act of man when, at the winter ingress, the curfew is sounded throughout nature. It indicates a spontaneous Promethean rebelliousness against the fiat that this recurrent season shall bring forth foul times, cold darkness, misery and death."

Ten minutes later I was stoking the fire as gleefully as Old Nick alias St Nicholas, patron saint of students (which may explain why he became a synonym for Satan). The flames, how-ever, shamed me by illuminating the rest of the debris. So, leaving the first fire, I lit a second. Now there is a knack in building and burning a bonfire; and without that knack neither the bonfire nor the building will justify its name. Paper and twigs must be dry, and the larger sticks so stacked that they create sufficient draught at their base. If the job is done well, it never misfires; if the job is done badly, it never fires at all. Although smoke may arise without flames, not Prometheus himself could coax flames without fuel. In other words, the first fire dwindled while the second leaped; and since the two were set twenty yards apart, the busyness of feeding them became warmer than the laziness of watching them. Fortunately, the twin pyres added inspiration to perspiration. It would be a pity, I reasoned, to spoil the clean-up for the sake of a ha'porth of paper and twigs. Thus it came to pass that a third fire arose, as it were thrice denying Guy Fawkes and Catesby and all other Scarlet Men, but without bowing either to Knox or to Praise-God-Barebones.

The frost meanwhile grew keener, the ground damper, the air colder; but not I. Coatless and tieless, I scurried like an ant, dragging wood for three fires whose hunger mounted in proportion to the volume of fuel that was heaped onto them. I still bear some of the scars incurred while stumbling over tree stumps, and scrambling through briars. I certainly gained a deeper insight into the afflictions of Job: "Man is born unto trouble, as the sparks fly upwards.' Yet the result justified the effort. What a spectacle those flames made! They daubed the wood until every tree quivered like a mast on fire. They belched columns of smoke scented with apple wood, cherry wood, and autumnal leaves. They crackle louder than a regiment of squirrels marching over brittle twigs and fallen leaves. They echoed William Dunbar's fear of Hell fire: "*Timor mortis conturbat me.*" And then, quite suddenly, instead of wading among felled boughs, I found myself scrabbling for twigs; so ravenous had been the blaze, such its intensity and duration. By the glimmer of the last flame I looked at my watch. It said midnight. For more than three hours I had hacked and hurried, shovelled and carted, prodded and ducked, sweated and shivered. Now at last the tidemark had disappeared, and the morrow would reveal green grass beside trim hedgerows.

By way of cooling off, I climbed to the brow of the hill, whence the Exmoor heights were visible, clear and near against the stars. There, too, on lower ground, a bonfire blazed, lit no doubt by a Protesting farmer. For a moment I fancied that my own trio had kindled the sort of nightpiece which Housman painted:

> From Clee to heaven the beacon burns,
> The shires have seen it plain,
> From north and south the sign returns
> And beacons burn again.

Cow with a Crumpled Horn

While my host was opening a window to admit the cat, he noticed a car entering one of the meadows beyond the garden. A Land Rover followed, and presently we heard some shouting.

"They can hardly be cattle rustlers," my host remarked. "Not in broad daylight. And yet . . ."

"Well?" I asked.

"The man who owns that land has just bought a valuable cow. They say he paid several hundred pounds." He turned to the window again. "Let's go and see what's happening."

It was cold outside, more like teatime than noon. A mist came up from the river, swirling like ghostly octoplasm. The trees were going bald. Only a robin sang, as though whistling in the dark. Having reached the meadow, my host recognised the car. "It's the vet," he explained.

Sure enough, we found the vet and a farmhand gazing at a dejected Jersey.

"A chance in a million," the farmhand told us. "She caught her head in the gate-chain."

"Is she badly hurt?"

"No," the vet replied. "Just a crumpled horn and a slight abrasion. But it'll sting a bit, so we'll have her indoors before I start."

While the vet returned to his car, the farmhand led the cow

back to the dairy. "Everyone's getting soft nowadays," he muttered. "My old father would never have fetched the vet. He'd have done his own first aid. But there it is. The boss was away, and I didn't fancy tinkering with three hundred quidsworth."

Although veterinary matters were discussed nearly two thousand years ago, in a treatise by Vegetius, the first veterinary college—at Lyons in France—was not founded until 1762. Eighteen years later a Frenchman, St Bel, founded England's Royal Veterinary College in London. Until 1881 the Highland and Agricultural Society of Scotland issued its own veterinary certificates. Like a doctor, the modern vet must undergo a long novitiate. Unlike a doctor, he cannot question his patients. Fortunately, however, animals are as a rule healthier than human beings, less subject to psycho-somaticism and premature decay. Spared the burden of a vivid imagination, they resemble Mary Webb's old countryman: "He meets death with the absence of morbidity—almost amounting to indifference—which you find in the gay, short-lived citizens of wood and meadow."

The power to heal is not simply a controlled experiment. In some people it appears as a gift, for while orthodox medicine fails, unorthodoxy may succeed. To call it faith, or quackery, or coincidence, may be to state a fact; but the statement *per se* neither confutes the cure nor uncovers the cause. Healing hands are not an illusion. A sickly calf, a wounded sparrow, a listless child . . . certain countrymen seem able often to alleviate and sometimes to cure, though they received no training, and can scarcely write their own name.

A deep chasm separates man from the rest of creation. Only a sentimentalist projects onto animals a sensitivity which they do not possess. Shakespeare put the matter bluntly in *Love's Labour Lost*: "he is only an animal, only sensible in the duller parts." Nevertheless, some kind of communication between man and beast is possible, as everyone knows who keeps a dog, or a horse, or a bird-table. More than a century ago Richard Warner observed the rapport among Cornish ploughmen and their oxen: "While the hinds," he wrote, "are thus driving their patient slaves along the furrows, they constantly cheer them with conversation, denoting approbation and pleasure." Such men practise the creed of Thomas Hardy, who declared that both human and animal pain "shall be kept down to a minimum by loving kindness, operating through scientific knowledge . . ."

The word 'animal' is tinged with irony because of its association with spirits or souls (Latin *anima*). One can understand why the early Fathers denied that animals are immortal. Even the most ethereal alligator would cause unease in heaven. And what of mice among the deaconesses? Richard Jefferies did not believe that animals possess souls, but he did believe that they consciously experience happiness: "The joy in life of these animals—indeed of almost all animals and birds in freedom—is very great. You may see it in every motion; in the lissom bound of the hare, the playful leap of the rabbit . . ." Unless they happen to be in a zoological mood, most people agree that a tail-wagging terrier really does feel pleased.

Few creatures were more faithful than the dog which stood beside the body of his master who had died after a fall on Helvellyn. No one came to search for the missing man. No one, it seems, knew that he had climbed the mountain. So, the dog stood beside his master. Several months later a shepherd found the dog, emaciated but still on guard. Wordsworth told the story, in a poem called *Fidelity*:

> The Dog, which still was hovering nigh,
> Repeating the same timid cry,
> This Dog, had been through three months' space
> A dweller in that savage place.

Keeping strictly to its own domain, and occasionally asserting that no other valid domain exists, science defines the dog's fidelity as 'instinct' or a reflex chemical reaction. Seeking to account for the reaction, Wordsworth offered the unverifiable answer of Christianity:

How nourished there, through such long time,
He knows who gave that love sublime;
And gave that strength of feeling, great
Beyond all human estimate.

Frost at Midnight

Starlight confirms Coleridge's prediction that the raindrops on his
roof would freeze before nightfall:

> the secret ministry of frost
> Shall hang them up in silent icicles,
> Quietly shining to the quiet moon.

But this is no ordinary frost. It is a Cumbrian frost, so keen that
even the fellsmen feel it. The air tweaks the tip of your nose and
then pinches the lobes of your ears. It treads on your toes, nips
your fingertips, shivers your spine. There seems no escape. The
fang penetrates everything, piercing walls of wool and layers of
leather. Each breath inhales it, blowing icy smoke rings.

Some of our frosts have made history. During the twelfth
century, for example, the Thames at London Bridge was once
frozen from December until March; and in 1281 the bridge lost
five of its arches, all swept away by ice floes. Four centuries later
the citizens roasted an ox in mid-stream while lightermen complained that another week of solidity would liquidate them. In
1776 even the south of England suffered an Ice Age. Writing
from his Hampshire parsonage, Gilbert White informed the Hon.
Daines Barrington that he "never before or since has encountered
such rugged *Siberian* weather ... During these four nights the
cold was so penetrating that it occasioned ice in warm chambers
and under beds." In 1793 an Exmoor farmer, John Thorne of
Radworthy, wrote: "The Terriblest Winter this year since the
one in 1776 ..." Even the hardy moorland ponies were at risk:

"forc'd to feed the Exmore colts . . ." White himself reported: "vast rime on trees all day . . . great distress among the flocks; the turnips are all rotten. The ewes have little milk, and lambs die." Such bitter spells still recur, as in 1963, when ravenous foxes hunted at noon through the centre of East Grinstead in Sussex. Nor are the rigours confined to winter. *Punch* long ago announced: "Spring has set in with its usual severity." Perhaps

Mr Punch borrowed the joke from Coleridge, who had used it in 1826. Perhaps Coleridge borrowed it from Madame de Sévigné, who had used it in 1689.

As spiders spin their web by secreting separate threads, so frost weaves each visual euphony into a single fugue. Frost, therefore, is a greater artist than snow, which, like a demagogue, merely suppresses or deforms, levelling down while seeming to level up. Snow deadens sound, but frost acts like a microphone, detecting whispers. When a shrew steps on a twig, the echo runs fifty yards; when a dog barks, the next parish hears it. The dynamics of frost may be stated as follows: after sundown the earth radiates heat, thereby lowering the temperature of the radiators—trees, roofs, grass—which in turn cool the air that comes in contact with them. If those radiators are sufficiently cold they will transform the air into moisture; and if the temperature falls below freezing point the moisture becomes hoar frost or ice crystals. A mild hoar frost will form crystals only on the ground, whence the phrase 'ground frost'. A so-called 'black frost' occurs when the temperature freezes but cannot form ice crystals because a drying wind has reduced the volume of moist air. When a hilltop cools the atmosphere by radiation the cold vapour descends, which is why summits sometimes remain frost-free while valleys are frostbitten. Clear skies and an absence of wind tend to increase radiation and with it the risk of frost. Coleridge, therefore, was misleading when he wrote:

> The Frost performs its secret ministry
> Unhelped by any wind.

Science can deepen our understanding of frost, but it neither enlarges nor belittles our wonderment at the thing itself, transmuting a landscape. Seen now at midnight under a full moon, the woods elude description. Language cannot paint the trees that wait like patient penguins, slashed black-and-white from head to foot. Language cannot measure the millimetres of lace that cling to twigs which themselves create a filigree against the stars. Language can only stumble over the briars that loop like the tentacles of a silver octopus. Language—if it did speak—would shatter the crystals that gleam like diamonds in an ebony tiara. Each object, and every part of each object, share the same frozen veneer, so that their patterns propound a fanciful geometry. Fields look as though they had been sprinkled with sugar icing. Water-butts dribble a stream of stalactites. Holly leaves seem to have been cut from tissue paper. Brooks are opaque glasshouses, filled with fish. Windows resemble webs spun by snowy spiders. As a spectacle, therefore, frost is peerless. As a cultivator, it helps the farmer to achieve a friable tilth by crumbling the clods. But there the good deeds end, because frost is nature's sharpest executioner, surer than disease, deadlier than drought, swifter than age. It embalms birds while they sleep. It bites root crops. It splices trees. It cracks metal.

Few folk are abroad at this late hour, and fewer still for pleasure. If a farmer does walk the fells, his own footsteps heighten the profundity of Thomas Hood's landscape:

> There is a silence where hath been no sound;
> There is a silence where no sound may be . . .

A Welcome to Winter

At the end of November we bid goodbye to autumn, and prepare to welcome winter. The reception is not a mere formality, as it was in March, when we met the spring halfway, having lain in wait since February's blackbird announced that the visitor had been sighted. Nor is the reception unnecessary, as it was in June, when summer arriving seemed indistinguishable from spring departing.

Winter's entry is altogether different. No one meets it halfway. On the contrary, we keep our door shut when the first snowflake confirms that the guest has indeed arrived. By way of postponing the inevitable, a countryman speaks of "an autumnal nip in the air", though he really means that frost has gripped the ground. He remarks that the nights are getting longer, though he really means that teatime is lighting-up time. Such pretence is harmless enough, and deceives no one, least of all the pretender. But a day arrives when winter itself mocks the illusion. Snow, perhaps, blocks the lane, or a gale strips the trees, or a burst pipe summons the plumber. The mistily mellow autumn of Keats has given way to bleak December, the start of a season from which very few Britons have never wished to escape, into Aegean sunshine or among Italian vineyards. Hunting folk welcome winter despite the inclemency, not because of it. Only the purveyors of rain-coats, electric blankets, and other seasonable commodities feel dismayed when spring arrives; and, of course, the really prosper-ous purveyors can afford to hibernate in Africa.

The prime difference between winter and the other seasons is not of scent nor colour nor sound, nor even of temperature. Those things are indeed important, both to me and to animals, yet they remain overshadowed by the prime difference itself, which is between light and dark, between days in the sun and evenings by the fire. Breakfasting by lamplight at seven o'clock of a November morning, a farmer recalls that at the same hour in June he was mowing a meadow. Groping through a wood at five o'clock of a November afternoon, he recalls that the same hour in August he was seeking the shade. "Summer," said Thomas Campion, "has its joys, and winter its delights." Chief among those delights is a warm hearth, as John Whittier remembered:

> Shut in from all the world without,
> We sat the clean-winged hearth about,
> Content to let the north wind roar
> In baffled rage at pane and door . . .

Firelight, however, evokes sunlight, or at least a vision of it. No matter how snug his hearth, a countryman overhears Shelley's question: "If Winter comes, can Spring be far behind?" Walter de la Mare was very frank about it. Firelight or not, he disliked what he saw when he peered through the window:

> There is a wind where the rose was;
> Cold rain where sweet grass was;
> Grey skies where the lark was.

Yet winter is not a penitential procession of dark days and freezing nights. A December afternoon in Devonshire can be milder than a May morning in Morayshire. A muggy mist can give way to a tingling snowscape. A shrill storm can be followed by a thrush singing from sunlit branches. Countryfolk need not look far if they would see the beauty of winter, nor do they often look in vain. Only winter suffuses the sky with that blood-red sun, shedding sapphire shadows on frozen furrows. Only winter paints those pink-coated horsemen, riding like robins over a dun horizon. Only winter evokes the tang of bonfires and new-felled timber. Only winter bares the woods to the bone of their boles, silhouetting each twig. Only winter spreads a white cloak across the earth, under whose folds everything assumes a new and magic beauty. Only winter unleashes the full fury of seas seeking a landfall.

When a certain lady declared her willingness to accept life, Carlyle muttered: "By God, she had better." So is it with winter, from which there are only two ways of escape, either to a warm climate or to a point of no return. The first remedy is expensive, and the second is irremediable. In urging us to love all the seasons, Coleridge did not demand that our affection be distributed among them equally. He meant rather that we must acknowledge the best despite the worst, weighing a red sunset against a grey dawn. Winter, after all, does not strike unexpectedly from behind, nor as a thief in the night. Like age, it confronts us, and can be seen far ahead. Did we not hear the first footsteps in September, when the lights went on while we sipped our port or washed our dishes? Were we not initiated last month, when Parliament compelled us to put the clock back? We have been given ample time in which to cut our summer cloth to fit a lean season; and the leanness advances gradually, unlike those Arabian nights that within a few minutes can transform sunshine into starlight.

"Byzantium," warned Yeats, "is no country for old men." Winter, certainly, is no season for faint hearts. Think of the shepherds patrolling the mountains. On foot they go, or astride a pony, up and up into mist and sleet and solitude. Think of the men who go down to the sea in ships; when Boreas blows, they perceive the wonders of the Lord in the deep; and for some of them that is the last thing they ever do see. Think of the men and women who keep the land and its animals in good heart. Bracing it may be, but few would call it a joke, to lug hay across three snowfilled fields, or hack ice from a cattle trough, or plough a wind-whipped furrow, or deliver letters down a mile of ankle-deep mud. Yet such are the daily tasks of those whom Whitman classified as "out-of-doors natural persons, men living close to the elements . . . "

Austere, rigorous, lit with moments of bleak beauty; that is the winter which countryfolk now welcome.

12

The Tweed and the Tailor

The jacket I am wearing was made fourteen years ago by a village tailor who in fine weather worked at an open window overlooking his cherry orchard. The jacket is of grey tweed, cut so capaciously that it would meet the needs of a horseman or of a poacher or of a walker who carries maps, books, pencils, tobacco, matches, dog-comb, and sandwiches. It cost me twelve guineas, and was at that time the most expensive ever made by the tailor.

Since I never grow fond of a garment until I have worn it for at least five years, the jacket remained merely an acquaintance until I happened to notice that the material was fading. This symptom of age affected me, as do the grey hairs on a friend with whom we heard the chimes at midnight. When the jacket was twelve years old I took to wearing it every day, knowing that even the best tweed is mortal. In the course of those daily adieus I recalled the jacket's first public appearance, which had taken place in front of a television camera, against a background of Westmorland fells. I recalled another public occasion—this time at Selkirk—when, prompted by Sir Walter Raleigh's more obeisant gesture, I set the jacket round the shoulders of Lord Home, who was then Foreign Secretary, to shield him from a shower. I recalled also the day when I slept on the jacket, lying full-length beside the sunlit source of the Severn on the summit of Plynlimmon. Finally, I recalled wearing the jacket in a blizzard that whitened the beechwoods at Bix in the Oxfordshire Chilterns, but failed to penetrate the tweed.

Charles Lamb mourned the declining number of London beggars. I mourn the declining number of village tailors. Such men are equable, industrious, and proud of their craft. They cater especially for the customer who, although he scorns to chase the fashion, does like his clothes to be handmade, with button-holes which open so that he can draw-back the cuffs when gardening. His jacket must fit comfortably, but without attracting attention to itself. On no account will it evoke Samuel Pepys's sartorial rapture: "Up, and this morning put on my new fine, coloured suit, with my cloake lined with plush, which is a dear and noble suit . . . " A countryman's jacket reflects the routine of rural life, unlike those non-buttonholed jackets that are imported from regions where men no longer pick a Sunday posy from their garden. Worse still are jackets with a riding vent for persons who have never mounted a horse, and would probably fall from a bicycle. One day, no doubt, the fashionable beau will sport an empty scabbard, or a pocket for his tinderbox. Brass-buttoned blazers ought to be a monopoly of naval and military men such as Thomas Hardy's patriarch on Egdon Heath, who habitually wore "an ancient boat-cloak . . . his brass buttons bearing an anchor on their face. One would have said that he had been, in his day, a naval officer . . . "

The decay of village tailoring is relatively recent. For example, there are certain very old people who once met Jack Russell, Exmoor's sporting parson; yet when Russell became vicar of Swimbridge, his parish maintained a tailor, a tanner, a baker, a wheelwright, three carpenters, and five farriers. The tailor who made my own grey jacket did not retire until the late 1960s, and even then it was a glut of years rather than a dearth of custom that caused him to set aside his scissors and thread. How nimbly he kept abreast of the times. When I last saw him he was at work on a pair of tight-fitting trousers for a garage-hand who in one week gave more to the brewers and the bookmakers than his grand-father had earned in a month of hard labour. But it was not the waste of money that irked the tailor; it was the expense of time. "That boy's mother," he remarked, "came into my shop one day. 'O Mr Taylor,' she said, 'can't you please make my Percy's pants a bit wider? It takes him ages to get them narrow things on and off. What's more,' she said, 'I have to press 'em twice a week for his guitar lesson.' " The tailor had weathered many changes of fashion. "Forty years ago," he remembered, "when Oxford bags were all the rage, some of the better class of youngsters could hardly have 'em wide enough. I once said to the doctor's son, 'If I make 'em any wider,' I said, 'you'll fall through the trouser legs.' " He smiled. "But there it is. Something new, something fancy. I dare say Adam himself thought it was time he wore an up-to-date figleaf."

The decay of village tailors is swift as well as recent. Only a year or two ago, while staying in the Cotswolds, I was advised that my everyday riding breeches, being then thirty-five years old, were inadequate and likely to become indecorous. At Chipping Norton, therefore, I went to consult a tailor whose window, a few weeks previously, had displayed various whipcords. Alas, the tailor was no longer in business. His shop had been "scheduled for redevelopment". A year passed, and with it my breeches, rent irrevocably. Finding myself once more in the Cotswolds, I visited another tailor, and with the same result. "You're a week too late," they told me. "Old Joe couldn't compete with the classy reach-me-downs. It seems a pity. Joe's dad made the squire's off-duty suits. Three quid they cost, for three pieces and a silk lining. And the under-keeper was still wearing those suits ten years after the squire had discarded 'em. No use looking back, though. Joe used to say that the factories turned-out a jacket quicker than he could thread a needle." Those two incidents reminded me of the tailor in Carlyle's *Sartor Resartus*, who sighed wistfully for "A day of justice, when the worth of Breeches would be revealed by man, and the Scissors become forever venerable." Mind you, the breed is not yet extinct. Here and there a country tailor still sits bow-legged beside an open window, making a suit of clothes as it ought to be made; every process done by hand, the buttons of real bone in real holes, chalk-marks on the cloth, and a fitting to follow. However, it is as well to be on guard against the tailor who still trusts his father's pattern book. In 1940 I asked a village tailor to make a second-best uniform, which he did, skilfully and of good material, but to a design that their Lordships of the Admiralty had jettisoned in or about the year 1918.

While Shepherds Watched

The shepherds that night were seeking a child, and scores of other countryfolk took part in the search, as well as three strangers who had lost themselves on the moor. Suddenly the strangers noticed a bright light, set so low in the sky that they exclaimed: "We've never seen a star like that before." Presently the light was joined by a red one and then by a yellow and a blue, and after that by green and gold. "It's a Christmas tree! We're nearly there." Comforted and reassured, the strangers steered by the star, delving deeper down hill, then over a stream, and at last to the tree itself, which stood in a tub beside the village hall. Several cars filled the forecourt, and others were parked in the lane, their rear lights glowing like a negative gantry. But the three strangers were not the only people who had almost failed in their search, for a farmer's wife was telling another: "We'm lucky to get yere at all. Six ewes broke loose just as we were leaving, and George had to round 'em up."

Inside the hall several rows of chairs were ranged before a stage. On them sat the parents, grandparents, and other relatives of the children who were about to act their Christmas play. The first row of chairs had been designed to fit the under-fives, but was now shared by the three late-arriving strangers, all of whom were over-fifties. On a table at the foot of the stage stood a framed letter, lately received from Buckingham Palace, in reply to a seasonable greeting which the village school had sent to the Queen. Amid some preliminary alarms and excursions backstage, the audience waved and nodded to one another, and talked of sheep, and mentioned a marriage, and feared an illness, and generally conversed much as their forebears had done while Duke William was winning the Battle of Hastings.

Sharp at seven o'clock the schoolmistress appeared on the stage. "This little play," she announced, "was first performed twenty-four years ago, and it's nice to think that some of our actors and actresses tonight are the children of the children who took part in that first performance." The teacher then drew attention to the Framed Reply, inviting the audience to read it. That done, she retired, and the trampling of feet off-stage announced the assembly for Act One. The lights were lowered, the last cough was stifled, and the curtain parted to reveal a mother and her son and daughter (average age ten years) decorating their parlour for Christmas. With professional unconcern they tied gifts to the tree while indulging some well-played domestic repartee which Mother nipped in the bud. "Now don't 'ee start quarrelling. Not on Christmas Eve." Through her spoke the very voice of Devon, pitched above parochialism by the knowledge that comparable companies were elsewhere uttering the voices of Norfolk, Ulster, Cardiganshire, Nottinghamshire, Croydon, Salford, Stepney, Caithness.

Turning from the tree, one of the children asked: "Mother, will the carol singers come tonight?" . . . whereupon a member of the audience (too young to be a member of the cast) exclaimed "Yes", and was at once justified by the entry of the singers themselves, the tiniest of the school tots (average age five years), each gloved and scarved against a frosty night. "It must be very cold outside," Mother remarked. "I'm sure you would like some cocoa." With prompt stage managership the cocoa entered, and not one drop of it was spilt. Thus inspired, the young voices sang the old words:

> While shepherds watched their flocks by night,
> All seated on the ground,
> The Angel of the Lord came down,
> And glory shone around.

During a pause for breath between the second and third stanzas, a very small member of the audience uttered a very categoric imperative: "I wanna wee-wee." Of course, any fool could mock the scene by presenting part of it as the whole. The women, for instance, eyed the women, as women do; and, as men do men, the men eyed the women. Any doctor could detect the chronic tippler and the hardened artery. Any layman would assume some malice, hypocrisy, gossip, snobbery. But only a fool would trouble to remark that sinners are not saints: *non angeli sed Angli.*

As the simple plot unfolded, mothers and grandmothers brushed aside a tear, and proud fathers applauded, unaware of the smile on their face. Soon the categoric imperative was led in again, through a side door, loudly expressing his relief: "I done my wee-wee." Next, a little girl stepped forward, about seven years old, named Sarah. Solemn as a preacher, blithe as a bird, rapt as her famous namesake Siddons, she recited a poem. Just such a child must have pierced Swinburne's twisted armour:

> Very sound of very light,
> Heard from morning's rosiest height,
> When the soul of all delight
> Fills a child's clear laughter.

So was told a Christmas story, a children's tribute to *the* Christmas story, which is itself the most beautiful poem yet composed by men; being both a legend (some say, an old wives' tale) and a myth (or symbol of intimations and aspirations). Time has modified most people's interpretation of that story. Lacking a verifiable pedigree, the Magi and the manger may one day disappear, even from the nursery. God himself may disappear, banished by a race of beings who have learned to live and die without comfortable illusions. At present, however, the Christmas story continues to exert a benign influence on tender minds for whom the infant Jesus seems as real as their own baby brother, and for some of whom, when life has scarred them, Calvary will seem as real as their own anguish.

When the final curtain came down, the shepherds and their friends agreed that the journey had been worthwhile. After refreshments and congratulations, the players and the audience departed. Lights were extinguished, doors were locked, and the last car burrowed its white way among black hills. But the Christmas tree remained, vivid as a midnight rainbow, and above it shone the star that had guided many travellers.

Making a Clean Sweep

It might have been spring because a primula was in bloom, and the sun shone from a cloudless sky. It might also have been summer because the garden was bright with flowering pansies, roses, dahlias, antirrhinums, and a couple of sweet williams. Light and warmth pervaded the house, revealing dust in the hearth and cobwebs behind the cupboard. But, of course, it was neither summer nor spring. It was a second Martinmas, carried over into December, fulfilling Shakespeare's weather forecast: "Expect Saint Martin's summer, halcyon days." Had he been writing for gardeners, Shakespeare might have added: "Days when the lawn is littered with leaves."

One of my own lawns adjoins a wood. As a windbreak, the juxtaposition is admirable. As a nature reserve, it allows me to watch birds from the study window. As a spectacle, it resembles a lagoon while May unfolds the bluebells, and a furnace while October kindles the trees. But when the autumnal flamboyance has subsided, I face the task of sweeping the leaves, starting with a dress rehearsal in November, followed by a positively farewell appearance in December. So, on this warm and windless day, I sit in the garden, complacently surveying a morning's work.

At breakfastime the lawn was littered with leaves. In fact, the whole garden was littered. Leaves were everywhere, in the tool shed, on the window ledge, under the doormat. They lined my gumboots, and had entered the pockets of an oilskin. In the gutters they caused an overflow. On the fishpond they floated like a Sargasso of perennial water-lilies. But now at last the debris has been collected and stacked out of sight, ready for burning. And in case any urban gardener protests against such waste of leaf-mould, let me remark that several centuries of non-clearance have deposited enough humus to fertilise several decades.

The best leaf-sweeper is a besom, a very ancient device, full of philological interest. The Saxons called it a *besoma* or bundle of twigs. Since the twigs were usually birch, and since the device itself was often used as a means of chastisement, the broom begat both a noun and a verb, 'birch' and 'birching'. In moorland country the twigs were usually broom, whence the common name for any kind of bristled sweeper. A besom must be wielded lightly and with a sideways action, rather as though it were a scythe. Thus used, it will gather the leaves without bruising the lawn. If you stab it into the ground, however, the broom will merely shorten its own life; and if you sweep during windy weather your folly will fly in your face.

When I lived in the Chilterns, my besoms were made by a bodger whose workshop was a tent in the beechwoods at Great Hampden. Once a year, in autumn, the bodger cut bundles of birch twigs which he stacked crosswise and lengthwise in a tapering pile that was thatched by other bundles, thus allowing the rain to soak away. In spring the twigs were seasoned and ready for use. Although besoms are nowadays mass-produced in factories, the craft is still practised by woodsmen. In Sussex, on the road from Battle to Hailsham, one cottager plies a brisk trade, though his chief occupation is trug-making. Last year I found a

Worcestershire besom-maker at work in Wyre Forest; another, near Wool in Dorset; a third, near Church Stretton in Shropshire. I believe that some of the gipsies still make besoms at their encampments on Icknield Way near the foot of Swyncombe Down in Oxfordshire. The technique varies from region to region, but all craftsmen bind their twigs on a wooden support or "mare" whose vice is worked by a foot pedal. The Chiltern bodger employed a timber vice, but in parts of Lakeland they prefer steel. Factory-made besoms are usually fastened with wire, a custom of which my Chiltern bodger disapproved. "A bit o' woire is wart oi call brittlesome. Oi wouldn't never use nothing but wood. Willow or hazel, or best of all bramble. If you do use bramble . . . well, see for yourself." He gave a demonstration. "Them strips o' bramble is thart strong you won't never break 'em. Go on . . . 'ave a try." I did, and failed. "See? Wart's more, bramble never gets rusty."

The broom handles are commonly of ash, or hazel, or lime. The butt end is pared to a blunt point and then soaked in water to ensure that it will swell. A really conscientious craftsman secures the head by inserting a small ash peg. The Forestry Commission used to provide rough-and-ready besoms for use by members of the public in helping to beat-out fire. But the brooms have been replaced by felt-like material fixed to a pole. Perhaps too many of the real besoms were stolen.

Woodwork is man's oldest craft. His ancestors probably studied it while swinging from bough to bough. By means of woodcraft he hollowed a canoe from a log; he hewed the cruck for a cottage; he carved bench ends; and he made Chippendale chairs. A besom, of course, is a lowly artifact, in no way a work of genius. Nevertheless, it fulfils the prime conditions of craftsmanship, which are comeliness and usefulness. If you suppose that anyone can make a besom, try to prove your preaching by practising it. If you ever do succeed in assembling the various components, I predict that some of them will fall apart after five minutes' brisk sweeping. My own first venture disintegrated while I was carrying it triumphantly from the woodshed. A second attempt held fast for a whole morning and then collapsed. Anyone can indeed make a besom, but only craftsmen can make besoms that look well, work well, and wear well.

Chips From an Old Block

Within a few weeks of taking up residence in his new home, the retired schoolmaster was dubbed "Mr Chips". His sister, who keeps house for him, shared the soubriquet, and became "Miss Chips". When the villagers discovered that she was a widowed grandmother they tried to adopt her correct name, which is not only double-barrelled but also prefixed with a "de." On reconsideration, therefore, they reverted to the spinsterly nickname. Some people define Miss Chips as "the very opposite of" her brother. Others, more perceptive, observe that she is his complement, for whereas the brother maintains a scholarly *gravitas*, the sister sits rather than stands on whatever ceremony is now deemed proper among elderly and erudite gentlefolk. But the informality never becomes familiarity. More than one intruder has been straddled by a "de" from the double-barrel.

The doctor, who fancies himself as poetaster, remarked privately that Miss Chips fitted Walter de la Mare's description of Mary Webb: "bright blue eyes, small hands, birdlike ... she loved to listen to others talking ... her own talk had an extraordinary eagerness and vivacity." More precisely, Miss Chips is slim and *petite*. She wears spectacles for small print, and remains so agile that, despite her fifty-eight years, she lately won the golf club's Ladies' Trophy, thereby capping her brother's prowess as honorary secretary of the beagles. Differences, however, do exist. Thus, while Mr Chips interests himself in hospital management and musical soirées, his sister is happiest when trying-out a new recipe for lemon curd, or reconciling the rich builder with the poor major, or judging at the flower show, or (as the sexton's wife expressed it) arranging a fête in aid of dry rot in the belfry. Miss Chips certainly shares her brother's tact and something also of his repartee. In her own drawing room, surrounded by members of the Women's Institute, she once gave a very frank reply when the local divorcée suggested that a Master of Fox-hounds be invited to address the group on Marriage Today. "That man," Miss Chips declared, "commits the seventh commandment with his neighbour's wife." Before the divorcée could spring to the defence of promiscuity, Miss Chips added: "And also, I am told, with another neighbour's niece."

Since Mr Chips never enters a public house, the vicar was one day surprised to see him lingering in the porch of the Saracen's Head. Surprise became bewilderment when Mr Chips, having removed his necktie, replaced it with another from his hip pocket, and then emerged from the porch. Not wishing to appear inquisitive, the vicar passed by, and still does not know that the discarded tie was a birthday present from Miss Chips herself, delivered with an imperative suggestion: "Charles, my dear, you really must move with the times. That Wykehamist tie of yours is at least twenty years old." Yet it would be quite wrong to suppose that the couple do not harmonise. After all, they like the same people, and dislike the same *bêtes-noires*. They rise at 7 a.m., and take turns at brewing early morning tea. Not being rich, they pool their resources; not being poor, they employ a woman who describes herself as "an obliging help". On summer Saturdays a farmhand spends a couple of hours helping to maintain the garden, which includes a sizeable vegetable patch and a notable array of rock plants. Brother and sister discuss Plato for pleasure, Miss Chips having got to know *The Republic* while she was reading Modern Languages at Somerville; but whereas the brother relaxes with Belloc or Montaigne, the sister prefers Jane Austen and *The Lady*. This domestic division of labour is the fruit of experience. Miss Chips, for example, never holds court between 9.30 a.m. and 11 a.m., when her brother is working at his monograph on

Housman's edition of Manilius. In return, Mr Chips never demands silence between 11 a.m. and noon, when his sister is sharing coffee and confidence with the village ladies. Their evenings, too, are equable; no television, selective radio, at least three undisturbed sessions each week, and so to bed at 10.45.

Miss Chips being an Anglican, and her brother an agnostic, their advice is sometimes solicited by villagers seeking the best of both worlds. Not long ago they received a midnight visit from a local girl who announced that she had "got herself in the way again," and had tried to solve the problem by swallowing a mild dose of poison. While Mr Chips showed her how to be sick, Miss Chips showed her how to be sensible; and an hour later Dad arrived, promising that all would be forgiven . . . again. Afterwards, while sipping a hot drink, Miss Chips remarked: "How up-to-date the Bible is."

She is the only villager who knows why her brother never married. His fiancée, in fact, was killed by a car. For several years the stricken man's friends hoped that he would find happiness elsewhere, but he is now sixty-five and so set in his ways that Miss Chips no longer arranges accidental meetings with suitable females. Concerning her own widowed state, all the village knows that, if she chose, she could change it forthwith. Her admirer is a spritely widower of sixty-seven, who lives at the Hall. Like Barkis, he has several times declared himself 'willing'. The vicar's wife was therefore dismayed when Miss Chips showed no inclination to exchange a thatched cottage for a moated mansion. Does Miss Chips remain a widow for her brother's sake? The major's sister says No. The Baker's mother says Yes. Miss Chips says nothing . . . or, rather, she has lately been heard to say how sad it must be for Sir Richard, living in that huge house all alone. At the Saracen's Head they are already placing bets on the matter. But the odds vary from day to day, according to what the groom heard and what the housemaid hinted.

On the Fells

Just before midnight the telephone rang. Drowsily dishevelled, he creaked downstairs, and lifted the receiver. "Shepherd here. Who? Thwaite? What in't world . . . hang on a mo." He drew aside the curtain, peering into the yard. "Hello? Thou's reet an' all. Thanks for ringing. Happen we'll cross on't brow."

He creaked back to the bedroom, where his wife was still asleep. The flakes were falling fast now, like small white paws pattering the window pane. He glanced at the warm bed, sighed, and said loudly: "Missus!"

She stopped snoring but did not stir.

He tried again, "Missus!"

This time she opened her eyes. "What's to do?"

"Young Jamie Thwaite's been on't blower. Theer's a foot o' snow agin Cragside."

"On New Year's Eve?" Missus blinked while she reached for her dressing gown. "What a time to choose."

"Aye," Shepherd agreed, speaking from the depths of a flannel shirt. "Happen th'Almighty made our climate on't sixth day, round about closing time, when he were feeling fagged wi' the whole thing."

Leaving Shepherd to tug at his socks, Missus descended into the kitchen, where she stirred the embers, scattered some twigs, and added a log. Five minutes later, sipping tea by the fire, Shepherd buttoned his gaiters. Missus—who was filling a flask—said: "Wilt be back afower daybreak?"

Shepherd shrugged his thornproof shoulders. "If the ewes came down far enough," he reckoned, "it needn't last long. But if I've to gang oop brow, happen I'll take a bite o' breakfast with Thwaites." He stood up, calling his Border collie. "Coom, Lass."

Missus opened the kitchen door, flinching from a swirl of snow. "Take care," she warned. "Thou's nobbut an owd man at last."

"Gie us yon tay," Shepherd muttered. "And then back to thy bed, else thou'lt wake more of a woman than's good for any man, young or owd."

"Oh, be off wi' ye then." She handed him the flask. "I'll hae the rashers ready seven o'clock as usual."

The shippon was very dark. Seeing a hurricane lamp, the pony stirred. "Owd man or not," Shepherd said, "we mun saddle oop,

Majesty. Theer's a flock o' shape sumweer, each one on 'em daft enough to lose her lamb afower she's dropped eet. So gie ower, owd fella, gie ower."

Inside the shippon the hooves clopped, but on the cobbled yard they were muffled by snow. Before mounting, Shepherd blew out the lantern, lashed it to a cord round his waist, and then moved off, with Lass pattering alongside, heaving up and down through the drifts. After half-a-mile Shepherd dismounted to force open a gate. Sheep were huddling under the drystone wall, bunched tight for mutual warmth. Flashing his torch, he began to count the flock, but was interrupted by a distant sound. He looked up quickly. "Geet her, gal."

Lass bounded away, loping into the darkness. Then Shepherd heard her barking. Several minutes later an icicled Herdwick stumbled into view, and floundered to a place among the fold. Up went Shepherd, his pony zig-zagging as the buried track grew steeper.

"Woo-oop, Majesty!" The trio halted, listening. From somewhere high above them came another cry for help. "Danged fool," Shepherd growled, "Gallivanting in a blizzard. Theer's no sense on't. Hoop, owd fella."

Away they went, growing whiter and fainter, until, beside a narrow beck, they found the ewe, wedged between the banks. Shepherd dismounted, lit his hurricane lamp, and set it on a boulder. More than ever terrified, the ewe began to struggle.

"Steady!" Shepherd cried. "Thou'lt not do eet alone. I'll gie thee a shove on't backside. Ready? Hoop . . . geet on, then, geet on. Dost think 'tis a game? Try once more. Hoop . . . hoop . . . " Amid a flurry of snow and spray the ewe staggered free. Shepherd turned to the dog. "Gal, bring her home."

Down they went, following their own hoof-holes. Soon the ewe got wind of the flock, and tottered towards it, safe though soused . . . a black sheep returning prodigally like a white apparition.

Once more the pony climbed, Lass to heel, while the torch carved yellow swathes through mounting drifts. Suddenly the dog halted, boxing the compass with vibrant nostrils. "What ee'st, gal?" The answer came inaudibly from a faraway lantern. "Nay, 'tis only young Jamie."

They met near the summit: two men, two ponies, two dogs, two lanterns.

"Jamie, I'm still twa short."

"Twa? Thou's lucky. I've a score uncounted. Aye, and feyther laid oop wi' bronchitis."

"Not to worry. We'll find 'em, Jamie. Theer's ne'er a shape on't fells as my Lass and thy Lil can't bring to boot. Best follow yon ridge. Happen they're caught in't slack beside the beck. I'll gang in a straight line and thee mun fan oot. And don't forget the steep bit t'other side o' parish boundary. An uncle o' mine fell in't the snowdrift there, and embalmed himself till a thaw came, three weeks too late to save him. I own th'owd fella was top heavy wi' beer. But even a White Ribbon might come to grief o' that bit of ground. Hoop again, Majesty!"

At three in the morning the snowmen trotted into Cragside Farm; their sheep found, their faces flushed beneath a white façade. Hearing voices, a young woman opened the kitchen door. "Jamie?" she called, peering into the darkness. "And who else? Garth Shepherd? Eh, but it's reet good to see thee. I've a bowl of porridge on't stove." An aged man joined her in the doorway. "Granfer," she said to him, "wil't luke to their ponies, luv?" Granfer nodded, glad to be of use. So, men and beasts shook themselves free of snow, and moved gratefully toward something more hospitable.

Inside a warm kitchen the girl surveyed her husband. "Jamie, lad," she confessed, "I'm glad to see thee safe."

Shepherd turned to Jamie. "When thou's been married as long as I have," he remarked, "she'll not be so glad to see thee. And yet . . . " he paused, glancing at the porridge.

"Aye?" said Jamie. "Yet what?"

"Yet theer's a bonnie lass James Thwaite, as'll hae the rashers ready seven o'clock as usual."

121